BOAT COSMETICS
MADE SIMPLE

By Sherri Board

Published by:
Lighthouse Press, Inc
P.O. Box 341668
Los Angeles, CA 90034

DEDICATION

This book is dedicated to Sue Jones for her patience in dealing with my abnormal obsession to clean boats, for her unselfish willingness to push a brush whenever I was in a pinch, and for listening to me throughout the writing of this book.

Also, to my family, who inspire me more than they know.

Special thanks go to my mentor and friend Bill Beck who has devoted his life to the maintenance of boats. He took me under his wing when I was an amateur boat maintenance worker which helped to develop me into the professional I am today.

CONTENTS

ACKNOWLEDGMENTS

I want to thank the following people who took time out of their busy schedules to offer their kind and expert advice:

Kathy Barnes
  (Illustrator and a great inspiration)

Bill Beck
  (Professional Boat Maintenance Worker)

Chuck Reed
  (Compounding and Waxing)

KC Underwater Yacht Service
  (Bottom Cleaning)

Odessey Marine and Diving Services
  (Bottom Cleaning)

Aqua Marine Sail Cleaning
  (Maintenance of sails and covers)

Jim DeBron
  (Cousin and proof-reader)

Lillian T. Manniff
  (of the Los Angeles Maritime Museum)

D.K.'s Donuts of Tustin, CA
  (The best company, coffee and doughnuts around!)

Peter Griffes
  (Publisher)

INTRODUCTION

My education concerning the cosmetic aspects of boat maintenance did not come about through reading books. Rather, quenching my thirst for such knowledge was obtained by asking questions of professional boat maintenance people, making mistakes and learning from them, testing products and finding the easiest and most efficient way of using them.

In writing this book I do not pretend to know all the answers; nor do I profess that my way is the only way. There isn't an "only way." I share these methods with you because they've worked best for me and I hope they do the same for you.

This book, then, is about the cosmetic aspects of boat maintenance. Everything one needs to know about maintaining the appearance of their boat. Following the advice in this book will not only maintain her value, but also keep her pleasing to look at and happy to board.

I would like to stress the importance of using biodegradable products whenever possible. Products used for preventive maintenance are a lot easier for our environment to digest than those harsher products used for restoration.

I have added a maintenance calendar to the back of the book. It is to be used as a tool in keeping your boat cosmetically beautiful. You will find by putting your boat on a schedule and sticking to it, that maintenance becomes quite easy.

Remember: The hard part isn't the preventive maintenance; it's the restoration after neglect.

Sherri Board (alias "Sher")
Newport Beach, California 1989

Welcome aboard mates. Stand by for your instructions.

1

TO KNOW HER
IS TO MAINTAIN HER

Sher's definition of boat maintenance: *"Attending to all her cosmetic needs because she deserves to float in beauty, not drown in ugliness."*

Before we dive into the how-to's of boat cosmetics, I thought it would be helpful to take a quick dip into some nautical history. My motive for doing so is to help you realize (if you don't already) how fortunate we are today to have the luxuries and safety features our boating forefathers did without.

By comparing her past to her present, we might better appreciate the great changes that have been made for our comfort and safety. Perhaps then we will forever treat her like the lady she is.

Floating Backwards

Pry yourself from your twentieth century boating luxuries, (whatever they might be: fiberglass, electronics, antifouling paint, etc.). Let your mind float backward into time and imagine that it's the year 1492 and you are Captain Christopher Columbus. You have just been given charge of three ships: the Santa Maria, the Pinta, and the Nina.

Even though the ships do not belong to you (they were purchased by Queen Isabella of Spain), the tremendous responsibility of this command is realized: without maintenance aboard, these ships and crew could not endure the demands of the sea.

So, being the incredibly ingenious captain that you are, you assign each ship the following men: painters, woodworkers, metalworkers, caulkers, and deckhands. This assures not only for the crew's safety, but also that the ships will return to the queen in bristol fashion.

Today your attitude concerning boat maintenance should be just the same as the intelligent Captain Columbus'. Whether you choose to maintain her yourself or hire a list of professionals, like Columbus did, all aspects of boat maintenance should be performed on a regular basis. As our seafaring forefathers said back in the olden days, "A ship is like a lady's watch, always out of repair."

Her Resume for Love

The words that follow are pieces of the boat's past. A partial biography that hopes to show you some examples of her growth throughout time. She has always been whatever seafarers have wanted her to be; this in itself qualifies her for much love and attention.

The Boat. Brace yourself. . .the boat does not have a baby book. No, as sad as it is, we can only speculate from crude drawings and a few phrases that the boat began its life millions of years ago as a log. And as news of the log traveled to different parts of the globe, people used whatever was available to try out the new invention, such as animal skins or clay.

Today, as you sit comfortably aboard your modernized boat, envision exploring the waters that draw you to them in a way that some of these ancestral boatsmen did: a caveman straddling a log; an Iraqi herdsman sitting on his knees in the middle of an inflated goat skin; a New Zealand aborigine balancing on a bundle of reeds; or as a Sindhi laying on his stomach over an opened-mouthed pot.

Sailing. It is quite possible that sailing was discovered around 8000 B.C., when an Eqyptian, floating down the Nile river in a Fayoum boat, stood up, spread his arms, and let the wind fill his coat and push him along.

Do you suppose this man would have traded in his coat for some Dracon or Terylene sailcloth? You can bet your sailcloth he would have.

The Bilge. At first, rubbish talk amongst sailors was referred to as *bilge*. But, one day long ago, some unknown sailor was sent to inspect the deepest, darkest, part of the ship where water and residue collect. After only a couple minutes in this black hole, the sailor was truly convinced that this area was also rubbish. From that day on, the area where water collects in a boat has been referred to as *the bilge.*

The Bilge Pump. Have you ever wondered how our boating ancestors removed water from the bilge without an automatic bilge pump? It is a horrible thought, isn't it?

An example of one way is through the use of a rotating, bucket carrying, conveyor belt. The system took empty buckets down to the bilge and returned them to the top full of bilge water.

The Head. Long ago, this basic necessity was located forward on the ship's beakhead which appropriately hung over a vast sea of water. Even though it wasn't the most private area to be in, the sea did a great job of reaching up and keeping it well washed down.

Anchor Cable Holes. Since her beginning, the boat has always been thought of as a woman. There was a time in history when she was consistently given eyes so she could see her way. The eyes were either painted on or carved into her bow.

But as time sailed on and the world modernized, the eyes of the boat changed their form, turning into the holes for the anchor cables.

Starboard. Years ago, all Northern ship's steering, which consisted of one oar, was located on the right-hand side of the ship, assuming one was looking forward. The steering side of the ship was first referred to as the *steerboard* side. Later, the word developed into *starboard*, meaning the right-hand side of the boat.

Port. When a ship came into port to unload her cargo, she had to bring her left-hand side up to the

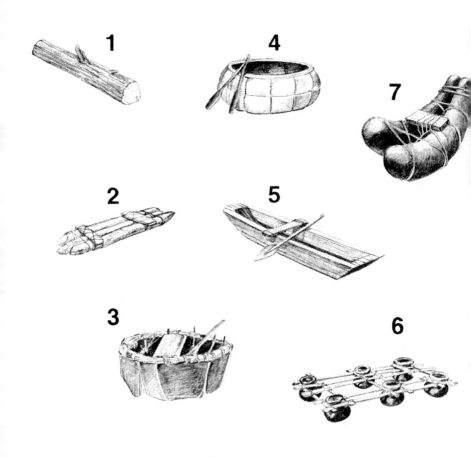

The Evolution of

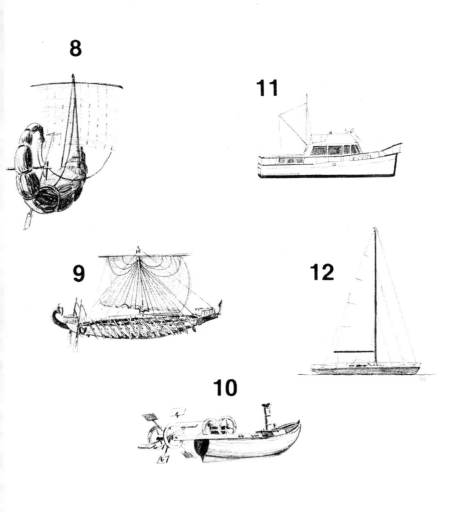

8

11

9

12

10

the Boat

docks so she wouldn't ruin her steering. The left-hand side of the ship was first called the *load-board* side; then later became known as the *larboard* side. The problem with larboard was it sounded too much like starboard and confused the sailors when out at sea. Finally, someone suggested that the left-hand side of a ship be called the *port side* - it stuck.

The Bow. Discovered by some Amazon tribe who realized if they streamlined the front of their dugouts, (i.e. hollowed out logs), they could cut through the water with less friction, allowing them to go faster.

Gangway. The opening in the side of a boat at the head of an accommodation ladder that derived its name from the term *gangplank*. In the days of pirate lore, it is believed persons who were no longer desired on board, like those who didn't do their maintenance chores, were told to *walk the plank*.

Maintaining Her Future

I can assure you, if you are maintaining your boat on a consistent basis, she will float proudly in recognition of the great technological strides that have been made, and will give you many years of enjoyment. But, if she's sitting somewhere neglected with her ego hurt, she is probably wishing she could go back to her simple life of being a log. This book will show you how to be a proud boat owner; not a mere bump on a log.

2

WASH DOWNS

Sher's definition of wash downs: *"Hardworking bubbles powered by elbow grease on a direct course to ensure her indefinite beauty."*

A boat should be washed down once a week and/or after each use. If harmful elements such as air pollution, salt and scum water, oxidation, and bird droppings are allowed to accumulate on the various surfaces, eventually they will become the proud new owners of the boat.

If you happen to be a busy boat owner, (perhaps you only have time for an occasional Sunday slip-sail), hire a boat maintenance service, or a neighbor kid, to wash down your boat for you. It would be cheaper to pay for the service compared to replacing cloudy eisinglass or sick looking varnish. Not only that, it feels better to board a clean boat.

Summer vs. Winter
Just because the boating season ends, it does not mean the maintenance program should.

Although it is easier to continue maintaining a boat in the warmth of southern latitudes, do not neglect her just because northern season's change. If your little toes are getting cold, buy some warm socks and rubber boots. If the boat is dry docked, pay her a once a month visit to make sure she is okay.

On a direct course to ensure her indefinite beauty.

Wash Down Gear

Limit the following items to wash downs only. Store them in a bucket or dock box for easy access. Ignore the desire to borrow something from your wash down gear so that the next time you are performing a wash down everything you need is there and not under a sink or flushed down a toilet somewhere.

[ ] Hose (as long as the boat)
[ ] Bucket
[ ] Hard and soft bristle brushes
[ ] Mild, non-phosphate detergent
[ ] 100% cotton rags
[ ] Chamois ("The Absorber")
[ ] Professional sqeegee
[ ] Elbow grease

Brushes

There are two types of bristle brushes I recommend for cleaning a boat. The first is a stiff polypropylene bristle brush which is good to use on non-skid and teak decks **only**. This brush can be found in most all marine hardware stores.

The second is a super-soft polyester bristle brush. Unlike the polypropylene, it is very gentle on gel coat, paint, varnish, and windows. Oddly enough, I have never seen this type of brush in a marine hardware store. But, I have found them readily available in motor home supply outlets.

Do your back a favor and buy a painter's handle or a telescoping extension pole. They are quite a bit longer than the ones found in marine supply stores.

Rags

When I think of "rags" visions of my little brother's holey T-shirts and outgrown Fruit-of-the-Loom underwear pop into my mind. Certainly these things do not have enough class to be used on our boats. And besides that, fabrics today are designed to repel water, not absorb it.

Years ago, faced with this dilemma, some west coast boat maintenance workers looked to the babies of America for the answer: **Diapers**.

What could be softer or more absorbent than what goes against a baby's precious behind? The diaper will do for the boat what is does for the baby's bottom: be gentle to its surface and absorb liquid.

If you have a diaper service in your area, you can purchase used diapers by the pound for a reasonable price. (Don't worry, they've been washed.) It is much cheaper than buying them from a marine hardware store.

If you do not have a diaper service in your area (or perhaps you have never heard of one), use rags that are 100% cotton. They will make your job a lot easier and, most of all, be more kind to the boat's surface.

Laundering Your Rags

I never gave much thought to washing and drying a bunch of boat rags until I heard about a fellow boat maintenance worker who didn't either.

My associate was doing what he did every Sunday afternoon; laundering his rags in preparation for another week of wash downs.

Everything was normal until the rags caught fire in the dryer. He realized immediately what he had done. He had mixed rags saturated with acetone with his regular wash down rags. Something he had never done before and never will again.

If you don't like surprises, keep wash down rags separated from all others. It is a good idea, and safer, to throw away any rags that might have harsh chemicals on them.

Fountain of Youth

Washing down a boat with soft water is like spraying her with water from the fountain of youth. Using regular water is like blasting her with water from the well of hard sediments.

Let us take a look down the well of hard sediments. It contains hard water filled with excessive amounts of minerals such as, calcium, rock, clay, magnesium, and iron. The severity of these lifeless matters depends upon the area you are in. Sometimes water can be so hard it will etch glass.

Everyone is familiar with hard water spots. These miserable crusty spots are just reminders that they dried faster than we did.

Installing a soft water system would filter out the harsh sediments, allowing you and your boat to last longer.

(**Important:** If you do use soft water, be sure you are using a mild detergent. Most heavy detergents are made to react to hard water - they may not know what to do in soft.)

Boycott Phosphates

If you are in an area that does not ban phosphates, you should. Phosphates speed up the growth of algae which causes confusion to marine life. Imagine being a school of fish whose path to education is suddenly cut off by a bunch of green bullies.

There are a number of non-phosphate, biodegradable detergents on the market that clean very well, such as Joy, Lux, and Wisk. Read the back of the container if you are not sure if a product is biodegradable.

(I realize some products recommended in this book are not biodegradable. That is because there are no biodegradable products to choose from for a particular job. But when these products come about that help us and the environment at the same time, I will let you know.)

Hose Down Surrounding Area

Before you start your wash down, hose off any dirt on the dock or driveway. This will give you a clean environment to start with and eliminate tracking the dirt back onto your clean boat.

Batten Down the Hatches

There is nothing worse than finding an open window or hatch **after** you have washed down, especially if the boat does not belong to you. Before you turn the water on check all windows and hatches.

Also, check the boat for obstacles that should not get wet. For example, it is easier to vacuum indoor-outdoor carpet compared to washing it off with a hose. Besides, a wet carpet is not something one wants to take on a Sunday bay cruise. Vacuum the carpet, roll it up, and put it in an area where it will stay dry.

Cushions and Control Panels

The following should be incorporated into your wash downs except you are not going to *hose them down,* you are going to *wipe them down.*

Vinyl Cushions: Wipe dirt and body oils off with a mild detergent and fresh water. Because these cushions absorb water like a sponge, do not flood them as if you are putting out a fire. Doing so will destroy the *cush.* And nobody wants to be without *cush,* especially in rough, open waters.

Closed-Cell-Foam Cushions: If you are not sure the cushions on the boat are closed-cell-foam, sit on one. If it feels like you are sitting on stacked BB's, it is closed-cell-foam.

These cushions are quite expensive but they pay back in durability. Maintenance is the same for these cushions and vinyl cushions with the exception that closed-cell-foam cushions cannot get water-logged unless there is a hole in them. They make great life preservers.

Control Panels: Wipe control panels off with detergent and fresh water. Do not hose them off for the sake of convenience. Doing so over a period of time could cause damage internally.

Where's the Water Draining, Mate?

Water exits a boat one of four ways: scuppers, bilge pump, pulling the plugs, or a bailing bucket. Make sure before you start your wash down that the water will drain from the boat and not fill up around your ankles.

I knew of an unfortunate boat owner who, unknowingly, hired a "flash in the pan" to wash his 18' Schock Electric.

Rather than filling a bucket up with water, Mr. Flash thought it would be easier to fill the boat up like a bathtub.

I am not quite sure how Flash got the water out of the boat, (he probably thought it would evaporate), but I know it was not by way of the bilge pump because when the boat owner went to turn on the motor the next day, the only sound that came out was, "Gurgle, gurgle, gurgle."

If the water has no way of getting out, don't put it in.

Topknot Dirt

I served part of my apprenticeship as a boat maintenance worker washing down boats for a broker in Newport Beach. Her office was on the second floor which enabled her to view the boats and any person on them.

One sunny April day I was washing down a boat for the In-the-Water Boat Show. As I was pridefully drying off the last water drop (I knew the boat would be the cleanest in the show) the broker yelled down from her balcony like a queen bee reprimanding one of her workers, "Sher, you didn't wash off the canopy."

I climbed up the side of the boat and stood on my tip toes. Sure enough, there was a layer of dirt laying on the canopy. I had to rinse it off and watch it destroy my perfect wash down.

Don't make the same mistake. Start from the highest point of the boat, check the top of it, and work your way down from there. Doing so will guarantee that dirty water will not cross a clean surface.

Mildew

This green garbage grows like the blob in warm, damp, dark places. It can usually be found on the shady side of a boat and normally appears during the humid summer months, invading the boat like tourists returning to their favorite sultry resort.

To combat against mildew, use X-14 commercial mildew remover. It will remove the mildew without any effort on your part except rinsing it off the boat when it is done doing its duty. **Do not get X-14 on painted surfaces.**

To prevent these travelers from returning, keep the boat clean, dry, and waxed.

(Bleach also kills mildew. It is harder to work with and can damage surfaces if it gets out of hand. If you are going to use it, dilute with water and keep confined to mildewed area only.)

Teak Trim/Decks

During your wash down, scrub teak decks and trim with a stiff polypropylene bristle brush. Scrub across the grain of the wood, not with it. Scrubbing with the grain rips out the soft fibers. Your objective during a wash down is to eliminate the surface dirt not the wood. (For monthly care see Chapter 4, Teak Tips.)

Defending Varnish: Enemy Overboard

If a varnished surface isn't kept covered, it is always battling with two bitter enemies: the sun and dew.

Their strategy is this: The dew, armed with acids and dirt, settles on the sleeping varnish and waits for its accomplice to rise. When the sun beats down on the dew, it magnifies the effectiveness of the dirt and acids, giving them extra strength to break down the varnish's resistance.

Your best defense for slowing down the breakdown process, besides keeping it covered, is to wash the dew overboard. This will render the team defenseless, sort of like Popeye without his spinach.

Swabbing Non-Skid Decks/Swimsteps

Sometimes non-skid can be pretty tough to get clean. Like after Uncle Fred spent the weekend dancing around the deck wearing his best black soled church shoes.

Use a mild abrasive like Soft Scrub, and go at tough marks with your stiff bristle brush. (Using a tougher abrasive will wear down the finish over a period of time.)

If the abrasive doesn't work, try some acetone. If those two don't do the job, call Uncle Fred.

Docklines

Docklines are like the brakes in a car. They are needed for safety reasons but not thought of until they start to give out.

Some time during your wash down, give the lines a gentle but thorough rinsing with a hose. Doing so will eliminate dirt, salt and river scum, which shortens the life of the lines.

Topsides

The topsides should always be done last because no other part of the boat will be affected by the wash down water running down their sides.

First, clean the waterline. Place your long handled brush just above where the water hits the boat and scrub down into the water about a foot. This helps prevent growth from forming and makes for a fine looking waterline. (The person servicing your boat's bottom should be doing this too. Read about this in Chapter 11, A Tip Top Bottom.)

Scrub the rest of the topsides with a brush, mild detergent, and fresh water. If it is a large boat, 32' or more, I recommend washing and rinsing off the detergent in sections so that it does not dry and leave a film.

If you cannot get to the other side of the boat to wash it, ask that it be turned around occasionally so you do not end up like the boat owner who loved his wash down service until he docked his boat differently and noticed the port side had not been touched in a year.

If you are pulling your boat out of a river or lake, be sure to wash the bottom with a brush, detergent, and plenty of fresh water.

Oxidation

If you notice a white film developing on the gel coat, it is telling you that it is time for a compound and wax. (See Chapter 6, Compounding and Waxing.)

However, adding about 3 tablespoons of vinegar to your wash down water will eliminate some of the oxidation. But only for the time being. Do not put off the inevitable.

Drying the Boat

The best tools to use for drying are a professional squeegee and a chamois, ("The Absorber" works great.)

Use the squeegee to pull the water off various surfaces and follow with the chamois. For large hard to reach surfaces like the topsides, attach the squeegee to an extension pole and pull away the excess water.

If it is hot out and you are using hard water, wash and dry the boat in sections. Otherwise, the water will dry on the boat leaving hard water spots that are impossible to get off. (Hopefully, you are on a boat that could be considered "a section" and you won't have this problem.)

Waterways: Normally after a wash down a boat will have some water build-up in its waterways, if it has any. Find where the water collects and dry it. If a lot of water is left over, simply pull it through the scuppers with your squeegee. If you don't remove this water from the boat, it will stain fiberglass and cause wood rot to a wooden boat.

Run the Bilge Pump

If you have access to the bilge pump switch, it is a good idea to run it after a wash down. Leaving water in the bilge could cause a lot of unwanted damage.

Check Interior

Always go below, if there is one, and check for leakage. Dry if wet. Notify responsible party before the leaking can cause permanent damage. Do not pretend water is not there. Crack windows if ventilation is needed.

Wings of Evil

During a wash down on a 32' Grand Banks I noticed these tiny wings on the deck that looked like queen ant wings. I thought, perhaps, queen ants were allowed the luxury of boating?

In my inquiries, I learned that they were not the wings of ants but of termites. I was astounded. I thought termites only had appetites for houses, not boats.

More often than not, when you notice these little creatures' wings, they have already made a main course out of the boat's cellulose. They shed their wings when they have found good eating and they do not plan on flying anywhere.

Call a professional right away. Do not wait until the termites become bigger than the boat.

Guano Got You Down?

For years boat lovers have tried to come up with new ways of discouraging birds from dumping on their boats. They have tried scaring them with owl figurines, snakes and corn brooms. Some have even gone as far as making an example out of one by hanging it by its neck from the rigging. (Not a very humane thing to do I might add.)

Being the perfectionist that I am, these scare tactics were not keeping my boats clean enough. I decided to use bird psychology.

Unlike man's best friend, a bird dumps in its nesting site, and the more it dumps the "sweeter" home is. So I decided that, maybe if I kept the bird bombs off my boats, the birds would go nest on the dirty ones. I was right.

I used a 22' Bayboat for my experiment because it was at the end of a dock with no boats to its port side and three very neglected boats to its starboard.

I washed the boat down weekly removing bird droppings from the covers and dock area. I was

Keeping your boat clean will help to prevent the birds from making a nesting site out of it.

amazed each time to find the boat clean while the others continued to get more and more dumpy.

The birds just sat on the other boats watching me, just waiting for the week that I would not show up.

Be Considerate

During your wash down, if you happen to get water overspray on a neighboring boat, be considerate and dry it off. This is especially important if it lands on a boat that is well maintained.

I almost lost an account because someone always left their water overspray on my perfectly dried boat. The owner couldn't understand why he always had hard water spots on his hull after I swore to him I was drying it.

Maybe if the next guy sees you doing something amicable, it will catch on.

3

DETAILS

Sher's definition of boat detailing: *"Refining the little things on a boat to enhance the beauty of the whole floating investment."*

Because all boats are thought of as women, maintaining her windows, stainless steel, cushions, etc., is like keeping makeup on her. If these "cosmetic" aspects are neglected, she will begin to look unkempt. (Remember: The older she is, the more attention she deserves.)

A once a month application of the following suggestions will not only maintain the value of a boat, but they will make her stand out from all the rest. The envy of neighboring boat owners.

A Note of Caution

You will get better results from your detailing efforts if the boat is clean and dry before you start. Otherwise, the various surface types may become scratched. As you are happily polishing a surface, the dirt underneath your rag will be viciously destroying it.

Schedule your monthly detailing tasks to follow one of your weekly wash downs. (See Chapter 2, Wash Downs.)

Windows

I will be discussing the proper care for the following types of windows: glass, plexiglass, and eisinglass. It may not seem important to treat these surfaces

Are you sure you are using a clean rag?

differently, but because they are so unalike, they must be.

Keep in mind that even though the tender-loving-care methods vary, the above surfaces all have the same worst enemy, **a dirty rag**. If there are any dirt particles in your rag, they will scratch and destroy all these surfaces quietly and unmercifully.

The sad part about the whole thing is that you do not notice the damage at first because the tiny, hairline abrasions are too fine to see. But after a million of them gang up on you, they will make you pay attention because you won't be able to see out of the window they have now claimed as theirs.

Glass: Of all the glass cleaners on the market to choose from, plain old vinegar and water work the best. They do not streak or leave a film of any kind. (Unless you add too much vinegar or the window is not clean.)

Pour one tablespoon of vinegar into a 32 oz. plastic spray bottle and fill with fresh water. Squirt solution onto one glass window at a time and wipe with a clean cotton rag.

Windows should be clear and sparkling. If they are not, there is something on them that should not be.

Plexiglass: Destruciton of this acrylic material comes from using harsh chemicals such as, ammonia or acetone, the sun and neglect. Ultimately, the plexiglass will become hazed and you will be unable to see out of it.

There are a lot of good plastic polishes on the market. However, I prefer Sea Power's plastic polish or Novus. Read manufacturer's directions and work substance in a circular motion using a clean, dry rag. Light scratches can also be rubbed out with polishing.

Do not use window cleaner on plexiglass. Most brands contain ammonia.

Eisinglass: This term is used for the plastic-zippered windows found on a boat. Because they are a vinyl, they scratch the easiest and deteriorate the fastest. As with plexiglass, the scratches found in eisinglass are due to dirty rags being used. Such an unruly common occurrence.

Eisinglass is also quick to show when it is being neglected. It will develop a milky white substance which is caused by the sun: oxidation. If this sign is ignored, eventually you will be unable to see through the windows. (I am sure you have seen some pretty bad ones around.)

A once a month application of a good plastic polish will keep the eisinglass looking great. If eisenglass is cloudy, use Novus plastic polish #2 to remove the oxidation. Follow-up with Sea Power's plastic polish.

A Bonus: Rain-X is a clear polymer which will adhere to glass, plexiglass and eisinglass. It repels water and foreign matter from it like a fly taking a crash landing on a sheet of ice. This attribute will make your maintenance chores easier and less frequent.

Rain-X can be found in most automotive stores. Follow manufacturer's directions on the back of the container.

Stainless Steel

Because of its unique characteristics, stainless steel is used quite predominately in the boat building industry. It is inexpensive, available, and virtually immune to rust and corrosion.

Most high-grade stainless steel can take a lot of neglect before it starts screaming for some attention. Do not let this trait keep you from giving it any.

Once a month clean stainless steel with a good metal polish. I recommend Brite Boy which has been around for years. I have compared it to a lot of other brands and I always go back to it.

After cleaning, apply a wax to the stainless steel. Not only will the wax add luster, it will also blend in scratches and repel water and foreign matter from it keeping it looking clean.

Pitted Stainless Steel: You will know if stainless steel is "pitted" because it looks like it has the measles.

The pitting is caused by impurities in the stainless steel, or low-grade stainless steel. (More is being studied on the causes of pitting.)

The most common areas in which pitting occurs are the following: an antenna base, fittings, controls, and stainless steel rings around gauges in a control panel.

Use the old stand by, Never Dull. If the pits are not too bad, Never Dull will take them down some. But for those that have been ignored, Never Dull will only disguise them for a while. Imperfect parts should be replaced.

Brass and Bronze

There is nothing more elegant than polished brass and bronze. And nothing more nautical than when they are tarnished. It is a personal preference.

If a polished finish is desired, a lot of work must be sacrificed to keep it that way. Although, if you want the shine but not the work, a clear coating can be applied to eliminate further oxidation. Also, applying a wax to the metals will slow down the oxidation process.

However, if the nautical oxidized finish is fancied, (that is the green or greenish-blue film that develops on the metals), no maintenance is required.

I know a boat owner who loves this "patina" with an added touch to it. He uses a 3-M Scotch-Brite pad, or "tuffy pad" on his brass hardware and scrubs off just enough oxidation to give it a brushed affect look. Thus creating the illusion that something is being worn. Like Aladdin's lamp, that only shined where he had rubbed so hard in hopes that his genie would appear.

Oxidized Aluminum

(Unlike all the other details in this chapter, this one does not have to be done once a month. Do only as needed.)

When the skin of aluminum is broken, it will oxidize and form a white chalky layer. This does not hurt the metal, but it is not cosmetically pleasing to the eye.

The aluminum can be sanded and a clear coating should be applied to cut the air off. Use whatever grit sand paper needed to remove oxidation.

Cushions

Keep a good vinyl cleaner/restorer on the cushions. If you do not, the sun will dry them out and they will crack like peanut brittle.

Do not use an abrasive cleanser or harsh chemicals on the cushions. Doing so will destroy the finish before your eyes. Trust me, I learned the facts the hard way. Years ago, one of my first accounts was with a boatyard in Dana Point Harbor. I was given a 32' Sea Ray that looked like it had never seen detergent and water. (It did not bother me because I was set to make it look brand new, i.e. create a miracle.)

To begin my miracle, I decided to start with the worst looking things on the boat, the cushions. They looked so filthy, I ran up to the marine supply store for some reinforcements: Comet, spot remover, bleach, and a hard bristle brush. After scrubbing for half a day, the cushions finally gave in to my drastic measures.

At the end of the day, the owner of the boatyard came down to inspect the boat. He looked at the cushions in shock. He did not hesitate to inform me that the layers of dirt I had scrubbed off the finish were actually the gray-blue finish of the vinyl. (I was fortunate he was so understanding, because it could have taken me two days work to replace those sticky-clean cushions.)

If you want the cushions to last forever, keep them below deck or have covers made for them. Keeping them dry and out of the sun will preserve them indefinitely.

If the cushions are kept outside, stand them up on their zippers. This will enable any moisture trapped inside to drain down and escape out the zipper.

Plastic Instrument Panels

If there is a plastic instrument panel on the boat, I hope there is also a cover for it. (An old towel or blanket would do.)

These types of panels take an awful beating from the sun and dry out quickly and crack. For its preservation, keep a good plastic cleaner/restorer on it.

Lifelines, Fenders, Shore Power Cords

Use acetone or lacquer thinner to clean all these items. Dampen a clean rag with one of the liquids and rub over the desired surface.

It may seem like you are removing some of the covering, but all you are doing is activating a thin layer of the surface. It will dry and go back to its original state.

I have used acetone/lacquer thinner on some of the dirtiest, I mean black, lifelines, fenders, and shore power cords and they have always come out looking almost brand new.

(Acetone/lacquer thinner will smear and erase names that are in ink on, for example, a plastic winch cover. Just avoid going over the name.)

Snaps

There is nothing more frustrating than fighting with a snap that is a million times smaller than yourself. On one particular boat, the snaps were so stubborn that when I went to unsnap the cover, the snaps stayed where they wanted, the material ripped from around them, and I was sent sailing across the deck. I was so mad.

Don't wait until you notice the little darlings are becoming harder to unsnap before you do something about them. Once a month, apply some petroleum jelly (Vaseline) or spray them with some WD-40. Doing so on a regular basis will help prevent corrosion and ward off potential tug-of-war matches.

Stubborn Stains

Listed below are three of the most common stains found on a boat and how to eliminate them.

1) Water-Run-Off: These stains occur most frequently in damp weather. The moisture in the air combines with any dirt that might be on the boat and

Lubricating snaps on a regular basis will ward off potential tug-of-war matches.

causes it to run down the sides. The constant flowing of these two culprits leaves behind an ugly trail.

Don't pretend you don't see these stains. If the boat is made of wood, they will cause wood rot. If fiberglass be the case, they will become as fixed as the Rock of Gibraltar.

Try a cleaner/wax, such as Sea Powers, on these stains first. If that doesn't work, use a very fine rubbing compound. Be sure that the compound is the same color as the finish. For instance, you would not want to use a brown compound on a white surface. After compounding, go over the area with wax.

2) Rust Stains: Not only are these stains ugly, but they depreciate the value of a boat faster than any other maintenance problem. . .unless, of course, you sink her.

Rust is the corrosion process of steel. It could be caused by impurities leaching from stainless steel, from hard water particles building up in one area (this is seen a lot around the base of staunches), from metal tools being left on the deck, and, perhaps, from someone cleaning their rigging with steel wool and the steel particles having picked your boat to land on.

Rust begins as a light brown spot. Remove it immediately. Do not wait until it is a "can't-ignore-it" orange.

There are a lot of good rust removing products on the market. If the rust stains are caught at an early stage, most commercial products will work. However, if the rust has been overlooked for a prolonged period of time, more drastic measures may need to be taken. Here are some suggestions that work well for me.

(A word of caution. The products listed below are very strong. Wear gloves and glasses. Keep chemicals away from your face. Contain substances to rusted areas only. If it gets on any other surface, for instance it starts running down the side of the boat, wash it off immediately with detergent and water. Read manufacturer's labels from start to finish.)

Muriatic Acid: Before you attack rust with this chemical, test a small inconspicuous area of the surface to be cleaned so you are sure the acid won't ruin the finish.

Dry rusted area to be treated with a small throw-away brush. Dip bristles into the acid right from the container it comes in. Brush the acid over the rust. If the rust doesn't disappear before your eyes, it has been neglected for too long and has permanently stained the finish. Flush area with detergent and water. Keep a dry rag by your side for unexpected drips.

Lime Away: (Test an inconspicuous area first for safety.) Lime Away can be found in most grocery stores. Purchase the spray form. Spray Lime Away on rusted area only. Let penetrate two or three minutes. Wash off with detergent and water.

Navel Jelly: You can buy Navel Jelly in any hardware store. It is a slower working chemical compared to the above, but it gets the job done. Follow manufacturer's directions.

3) Transom Exhaust Stains: Washing the transom with detergent and water after each use will prevent exhaust stains from occurring.

Rust Colored: Fill a plastic spray bottle half way full with muriatic acid and the other half with fresh water. Because acid may soften paint, spray solution on an unseen area first to test it. When you are **sure** it won't harm the finish, spray the stained area lightly. The rusted exhaust stain should disappear. Flush area with plenty of detergent and water. Re-wax.

Black Soot: Try detergent and water first using lots of elbow grease. If that does not work, a fine rubbing compound should. Soot contains solvents that may dissolve the wax. Re-wax when the stain is gone.

Also, a good running diesel engine normally burns clean and does not leave behind a horrible reminder that the boat had been taken out. You might want to check it.

Stain Prevention

Because oxidation and moisture help stains to develop, keep your boat clean, dry, and waxed.

Coiling your dock line is an important safety feature and looks nice and nautical too.

Topside Scuffs

These marks are nothing more than terrible eye sores. They are caused when the boat hits the side of the dock as it comes into its haven.

Acetone/lacquer thinner work great on these monsters. Rewax after removing.

To help preserve the topsides and the dock, "dock wheels" are recommended. (For the novice boat owner, we will call them "training wheels".) Keep them clean with acetone or lacquer thinner.

Dock Lines

Part of your monthly detailing duties should be checking the dock lines for the following:

1) Worn out lines. For security reasons, replace lines that are feazing. Do not wait until the Harbor Patrol calls you to let you know your boat is floating away.
2) Tension. If drawn too tight, they could snap.
3) Coiled dock lines. It is not only a safety feature, but it looks nice and nautical, too. (See illustration on opposite page.)

Shoes

Any shoes walking around on the deck of a boat should have white soles with very small grooves in them.

Shoes with dark soles leave hard-to-clean marks on the deck. And shoes with deep grooves may have dirt particles caught in them that will scratch the finish. (Some "boat shoes" are the worst offenders of deep grooves.)

Give a Darn, Lend an Arm

Some people do not pay any attention to the wise owl that says "Give a hoot, don't pollute." It is because of these deaf, uncaring people that we mariners must "Give a darn and lend an arm."

Simply pick a piece of water and claim it as yours. Keep a fish net, or the like, in the boat and when you see some garbage float into your space, fish it out.

I am not saying you have to do it everyday. Add it to your detailing list. It is not too much to ask to help keep something beautiful that gives us so much pleasure. Why take something so good for granted? Especially when it asks nothing from us.

Give a Darn-Lend an Arm

4

TEAK TIPS

Sher's definition of teakwood: *"The only wood that can be left unprotected against a harsh marine environment and still weather the storm."*

In the boat building industry, when it comes to laying the decks, attaching the trim, and securing the handrails, teakwood has the best qualities for the job. It contains a natural oil which makes it virtually rot resistant; it has high tolerance to an abusive marine environment; and it is pleasing to look at, even with age.

Because of teak's many fine characteristics, you may think that it is heaven sent. It is not. It is imported from the Far East. And even though teak can take it, it will last longer and look better if you give it some tender-loving-care whether you leave it natural or apply a dressing to it.

Leaving Teak "Bare"

When teak is young and first introduced into the marine environment, it is yellowish-brown in color. If it is allowed to weather naturally (without applying chemicals to it) the natural oils in the wood will oxidize, turning the surface a beautiful silvery-buff.

Unfortunately, keeping this silvered-virgin patina does not come without a price. It is one that can only be kept in a near perfect environment. Lots of foot traffic, oily hands, salt water, and pollution stain the teak, turning the silver into black. However, if you are

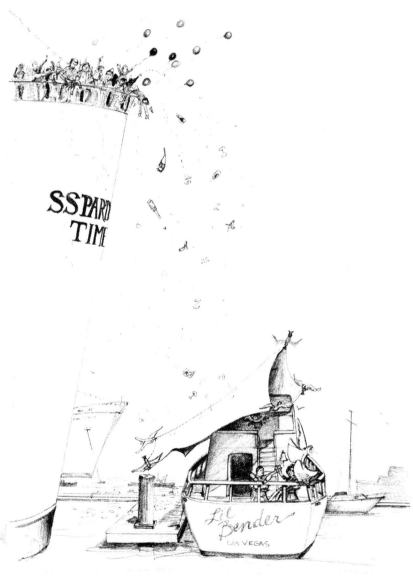

Keeping the environment off teak will help to keep it in its natural silvery buff.

in an area where you can keep the environment off the teak, the silvery-buff will wear well.

Sometimes it is hard to tell if natural weathered teak is clean or dirty because of the silver tint. If you are not sure, wet the teak. If it turns a golden-brown, it is clean. If it turns black, it is dirty.

(Remember: When it is necessary to remove light surface dirt only, do so gently and scrub cross-grain, not with the grain.)

A Bare Nightmare

We were maintaining a 42' Spoiler with four different levels of teak decking. The owner preferred us to leave the decks bare even though he enjoyed entertaining on a regular basis.

What fun we had cleaning and bleaching those teak decks just before every party to eliminate the chip and dip stains from the last one.

It didn't make sense to us that the owner chose to have his decks cleaned and bleached every week instead of having us put a dressing on them which would have saved him lots of money and decking.

We wonder, to this day, if that boat owner ever realized those potato chips cost him a fortune?

"Dressing" Teak

Don't be foolish like the boat owner above. Unless you are able to keep your boat in a clean dome-like setting (or you like the looks of potato chip stained teak), protect and preserve the teak by applying a dressing to it.

Teak dressings come in two forms: an oil or a sealer. The difference between the two is an oil penetrates deep into the wood, whereas a sealer remains on top of the wood, sealing only the surface pores. Both are quite effective. However, the decision to dress the teak is a far easier one to make compared to standing in front of rows upon rows of different teak dressings, mouth agape and clueless.

For this reason, I decided to compare the top seven dressings, three oils and four sealers, in hopes of helping the consumer before he pays the high price, apply the dressing and then realize perhaps, that he doesn't care for the way it makes the teak look.

Feeling like a cross between myself and David Horowitz, I based my study on color, ease of application and finish. Here are my results.

H.A. Calahan's Teak Oil: If you like the natural yellowish-brown color of teak, you will like this oil. Because Calahan's contains a sunscreen, it allows the surface to stay close to its original color. It also contains an anti-fungus agent and is easy to apply. It has a nice soft finish.

Mirror Glaze 46 Gold Teak Oil: This oil does just what the name implies. It leaves the teak with just a hint of gold to it. It is easy to apply and has a light golden finish.

First Mate Marine Teak Oil: Turns teak a burnt-orange color. It comes out of the can thick which might cause you to apply too much. Be careful of "globs". Finish is dark and somewhat dull.

Boat Life Teak Brite Sealer: (Has an "adult proof" cap. Have a sharp pick or screw driver handy.) Turns teak a walnut-brown and darkens the grain. Easy to apply, once you get through the cap! Has a warm finish to it.

Teak Wonder Sealer: This sealer leaves teak rusted-yellow in color. Application is easy, like applying rusted water. Contains silicones which hinder varnish. The finish is debatable.

Tip Top Teak Sealer: (Another "adult proof" cap.) Turns teak a cherry color. Easy to apply. Finish has just a hint of a pleasant red.

Watco Sealer: Gives teak a dark walnut tone. It is "sappy" to apply and care must be taken not to apply too much at one time. The finish is shiny and dense.

How and When to Apply

If you do not want your eyes to water and your head to ache for days, only apply dressings when there is plenty of ventilation.

I prefer applying a dressing with a brush as opposed to a rag because it does not leave behind lint or get caught on any snags that might be in the wood.

Watch for drips and wipe them up when they are wet because you won't be able to when they have dried.

Here on the west coast, we clean the light surface dirt off the teak, let it dry and apply a dressing once a month. However, if you are in an area where the ultra-violet rays are not as strong, or your boat is stored inside, you can wait as long as three to four months.

Bleaching Teak

Have you ever gotten stung by a hypocrite? Like finding out the down-and-out guy you just lent five-hundred dollars to is really living on his yacht in Mexico?

Bleach plays the same deceitful game. You think the stuff is wonderful because it turns ugly discolored teak back into its natural yellowish-brown. But you do not realize that while it is making you happy, it is destroying the teak's natural oils and ripping out its hard grain leaving it soft.

I am not saying not to bleach teak, just realize it is not all it is cracked up to be and should be done as little as possible, like lending people money.

Bleaching should only be done when detergent (biodegradable), elbow grease, and a Scotch Brite pad will not remove the stains.

There are a number of two-part cleaning and bleaching chemicals on the market. Read the instructions on the back of the container. Before starting the bleaching process, make sure the wood is clean so nothing stands in the way of the bleaching action and soap down all areas bleach may run across.

Bleached to a Pulp

I want to share with you a story about a boat owner who believed totally in bleaching his teak, until the day there wasn't any left to bleach.

This boat owner went through boat detailing services like a change of clothes. When the old got off his boat and the new got on, he would have them clean and bleach the teak. (It was like a test they had to pass before they could maintain his boat.)

When it came around to being our turn to maintain his boat, the teak was so bad you could put a screwdriver through it. I refused to bleach his "pulp" and he just could not understand how it got that way? All the wood had to be replaced.

Steam Cleaning Teak?

Although I searched for the perfect answer to this controversial subject, I did not find one. I talked to professionals who had both good and bad to say about it.

I have concluded that steam cleaning is quite harsh and could be detrimental to the teak. It should only be thought of as a last resort.

If there is something ingrained in the teak that you cannot get out by cleaning and bleaching, or through a water soluble paint/varnish remover, call a professional.

Check out the professional's references, ask questions, and get a guarantee. **Do not try to do it yourself.**

5

VARNISHING

Sher's definition of the art of varnishing: *"Enduring the tormenting details, so you can appreciate the beauty that springs from your meticulous labors."*

In waterfront taverns across the country, how-to-varnish is one of the most controversial subjects discussed among amateur and professional varnisher's alike. A dozen methods are exchanged over a dozen sunsets, but there are no absolutes.

Varnishing is one of those skills in life anyone can acquire if he masters the fundamentals. Once the fundamentals are learned, he will develop his own style; a way of doing things that work best for his personality.

This chapter contains the essentials of varnishing over teak wood. (Other types of wood, such as mahogany, demand the use of different methods.) **Do not** be in a hurry to learn and perfect them. Perfection is the result of much time and practice. **Remember:** Even the professionals had to start out as amateurs.

Check the Weather Forecast

Even though it is your time and sweat invested in producing a perfect varnished finish, Mother Nature determines what the final results will be.

Let's say the past two days have been bursting with perfect varnishing conditions. You have scraped and sanded happily (is that possible?) knowing the third day will bring the same wonderful conditions that will dry your varnish to a mirror finish.

Remember: Mother Nature has the final say.

On the third day, as you are applying the final brush load of varnish, a threatening, dark-gray cloud hovers over your boat.

You look up in disbelief. As raindrops start falling like little missiles on your unskimmed, tacky varnish, you know you are experiencing a reality: Mother Nature's punishment for not checking with her first.

Avoid unnecessary failures. On the morning you want to prepare or varnish a surface, listen to a local weather station for an up-to-date forecast.

Ideal Weather Conditions
Overcast, dry air, temperature rising, no wind, 60° to 70° F.

(Along with the above conditions, it is a good idea to varnish right after a rain storm because the air has been washed clean.)

Unfavorable Weather Conditions
A sudden temperature drop, rain, wind, excessive heat. (How these conditions affect your varnish are discussed under the heading Diseased Varnish.)

Don't Get Caught With Your Varnish Down
When preparing a surface to receive a coat of varnish, only uncover what you can cover the same day. Do not leave bare wood exposed to the outside elements for any prolonged period of time.

For example, imagine how much exposed wood you would have if you spent a week stripping and sanding it.

Now, assume the grand day comes when it is time to flow the first coat of varnish across that perfectly faired surface. As you are pouring thinner into the varnish, the good Lord is pouring rain onto your prepared surface. You pack it in because you know you can't varnish in the rain.

It pours rain for a week on your exposed wood. The weather has gotten under its smooth surface and ripped out the soft grain. Dirt and mildew have formed, darkening the wood.

Knowing you cannot varnish over mildewed, sand-blasted wood, you fall to the deck of your boat defeated. The truth hurts: You have got to start over!

What Condition is the Varnish In?

Listed below are three conditions typical of a varnished surface. The fourth situation is wood that has been oiled but is now under consideration to be varnished.

Read these descriptions and determine which category your varnished or oiled wood falls under. Follow the correct preparation method succeeding each interpretation.

1) **Well-Maintained**

The only imperfections in this varnish may be some nicks and/or dings, which can be easily eliminated. The surface may be slightly dulled: an indication it needs a coat of varnish.

Surface Preparation: #220-Grit Method page 53.

2) **Salvageable**

This varnished finish has a lot of flaws, but can still be salvaged. The surface is covered by small-spidery lines, some black spots breaking through the varnish and is dull and yellowing.

Surface Preparation: #60-Grit-Knockdown pages 53,56.

3) **Has To Be Stripped**

Time, neglect and the ultra violet rays of the sun have christened this varnish "Beyond Repair." It is lusterless, menacing, and harmful to the eyes. The only thing paying attention to it is the weather.

Surface Preparation: Varnish Stripping Methods pages 56-58.

4) **From Oil To Varnish**

Yes, you can switch from oil to varnish. The important question to ask yourself is, "Did the oil you were using contain silicones?"

If so, the silicones will react to the varnish like oil to vinegar, they don't mix. The varnish won't adhere to the wood.

Also, you may have to sand a considerable amount of wood away to get down to some clean wood again.

But it can and has been done successfully.

Surface Preparation: Cleaning and bleaching wood pages 58-59.

Sandpaper

For all the above surface preparations, you will be using sandpaper. Heed the following advice:

1) Purchase a good quality sandpaper which contains aluminum oxide. Keep your surface and paper dry. If the sandpaper gets wet and you continue sanding with it, you will create small aluminum scratch-like lines in your surface. You won't notice them until it is too late. They will be smiling up at you through what you thought to be your best varnish job ever.

2) Wet or dry sandpaper? The biggest difference in these two papers is expense. The wet sandpaper is quite a bit more than the dry. But the end result is the same. Both prepare the surface to receive the applied finish.

A good time to use the wet sandpaper is when there is a lot of dew in the air and on the surface, and you know it won't burn off until later.

Using the wet sandpaper enables you to get the damp surface prepared in time to get a coat of varnish on whereas you could not with dry paper.

Another great advantage to using wet sandpaper is, because you are using water, it allows you to see what your surface will look like with the next coat of varnish. You will know if the water doesn't temporarily hide the flaws, the varnish won't permanently. (Also, wiping the surface with a thinner rag will show any imperfections.)

Never prep bare wood with wet sandpaper.

Folding Sandpaper Effectively

To avoid making a fool of yourself, be sure when you are sanding that you keep the rough surfaces of the sandpaper from rubbing against one another. It is really quite easy. Follow directions on pages 54-55.

Following these instructions will give you approximately, a $5\frac{1}{2}$" x $4\frac{1}{4}$" piece of sandpaper to work with. This size is excellent for large surfaces such as handrails, toerails, and bulkheads.

For smaller surfaces such as small pieces of trim, take a quarter of a piece of sandpaper and follow the same folding instructions. This will give you better control of the paper which reduces the chances of scratching gel coat or paint.

Hand Sanding Block/Electric Sander

Not only does using a sanding block or electric sander give your hand a break, they also produce a more flat surface. I recommend using them on large, flat surfaces, leaving the smaller pieces of trim to be done by hand.

Because of the speed of an electric sander, a young man thought he could save time and make more money by using it on some small pieces of trim.

Standing back to admire his work, he noticed he had added a new look to the boat: tiny swirl-like marks scratched into the gel coat, compliments of the electric speed block.

It not only cost him more time, but also ended up costing him money. A very expensive boo-boo.

Varnishing Preparation Methods

You might not appreciate this rule of thumb but: **Preparation is ninety-nine percent of the finished product.** And for most, **the biggest pain in the neck.**

As much as you want to hurry through it, don't. Take your time and pay close attention to details. A clean, perfectly faired surface is going to give you a much better finish than a dirty, rough one.

Remember also: Uncover only what you can cover in the same day. My mentor, Bill Beck, has a fail-safe method he uses religiously (unless, of course,

Mother Nature has a mood swing). He prepares in the morning and washes down the prepared surfaces before he goes to lunch. When he returns, the surfaces are dry and ready for varnish.

#220-Grit Method

1) Clean any nicks or dings with thinner; lightly sand the imperfect areas with #220-grit sandpaper. Be careful not to expose underlying wood.

2) Clean sanded areas with thinner and apply a coat of varnish. Keep applying coats, being sure to let the varnish dry and sand in between each new coat, until the spot is level again with the surrounding finish.

3) After bandaged areas are dry, sand entire surface which is to receive the coat of varnish. This means you will be sanding over fixed areas again. Use #220-grit.

4) Because this varnish is in such good condition, you do not want to remove it. Only create "tooth" so the new varnish has something to stick to. The sanded surface should look like a sanded surface. No shiny spots.

5) After sanding, see Clearing the Decks, on pages 59-60.

#60-Grit-Knock-Down Method

This method is used to preserve a varnished finish one last time before it has to be stripped.

1) Yellow-air Pockets: These imperfections are merely voids in the varnish. Simply take a sharp razor blade, or pin, and poke a small hole in the top of the air pocket. When you flow your first coat of varnish across it, it will fill and disappear.

2) Black Spots: These are blackened areas which have broken through the varnish. Clean area with thinner and sand with #60-grit sandpaper. If the discoloration does not disappear with sanding, stop. Do not sand a hole in the wood so you have a crater to fill.

1

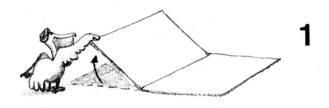

2

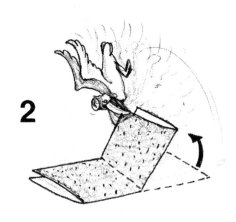

3

Don't be a nerd,

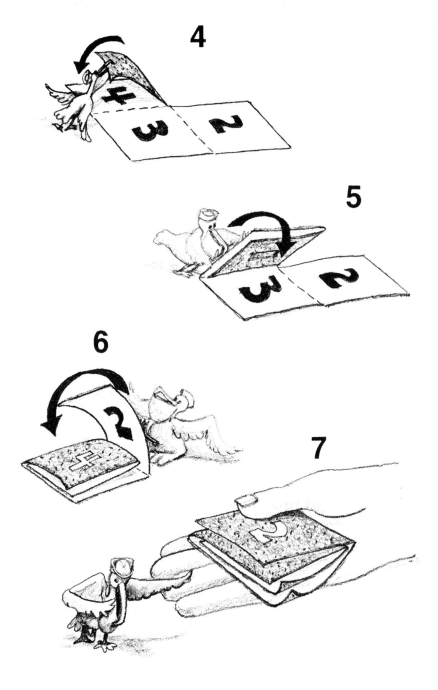

follow the bird.

Instead, see cleaning and bleaching wood on pages 58-59.

3) Wipe over areas with thinner. Varnish just those areas mended. Keep adding coats until the spots are back up to the level of the surrounding finish. Be sure to let the varnish dry in between coats and sand with #220-grit sandpaper.

4) When you have a dry, even surface, sand entire area to be varnished with #60-grit sandpaper. You want to really "knock" that old varnish down: eliminating spidery lines and dull finish.

5) Because #60-grit is so course, it will leave unwanted scratches in your finish. Sand entire area again using a finer sandpaper, such as #120-grit, and finish with an even finer course paper-#220.

6) After sanding, see Clearing the Decks on pages 59-60.

Varnish Stripping Methods

Listed below are three of the most common methods used for stripping varnish. Find the style that works best for you. If none do, use a stick of dynamite!

1) **Dry Scraping:** (Best method for thick varnish.) When using a *hook* scraper, it is very important to keep the blade sharp. Keep a scraper file handy at all times. You will know when it is becoming dull because it seems to takeover. It will veer off course and leave a permanent "smile" in your wood as if to say, "Ha, Ha, Ha!"

2) **Paint/Varnish Remover:** Most of these types of chemicals are very powerful. Wear gloves and keep your hands away from your face.

In addition, paint/varnish remover will weaken gel coat and obviously, the paint. If you lose control of the matter, and it lands on forbidden territory, rinse it off immediately.

Apply your first coat of remover to the area you wish to strip. After is has stopped bubbling, leave it on and apply a second coat over it. Wait until this coat stops bubbling and remove the lifted varnish with a sharp putty knife. Put waste into a container that can be sealed and disposed of properly.

Do not leave the remover on longer than necessary. Flush stripped area with fresh water and detergent to neutralize the substance. Because the chemical will leave your boat by way of the scuppers, thoroughly wash and rinse down the topsides. (Although this method is messy to work with, it is quite effective and will remove most all traces of varnish from the wood.)

When stripping is complete and all traces of the remover have been washed off the boat, the wood should be cleaned, bleached and sanded. See Cleaning and Bleaching Wood on page 58.

3) **Heat Gun Method:** I like this method the best because it is faster than dry scraping and not as messy as paint/varnish remover.

The most important thing to remember about using a heat gun is that it will break glass, soften gel coat, and lift paint. Therefore, keep heat away from vulnerable areas.

What you will need is a hook scraper (preferably with a wooden handle) or a putty knife. And you will need a heat gun. Heat guns are expensive but worth the price.

The process is very simple. The heat from the heat gun softens the varnish and the scraper removes it from the surface. With practice, you will be able to work the heat gun just ahead of the scraper at the same time and speed.

Be aware at all times where you are pointing your heat gun if it is on!

After stripping surface with the heat gun and scaper/putty knife, sand with #80-grit sandpaper to eliminate any leftover pieces of varnish and then clean and bleach.

4) **Cleaning and Bleaching Wood:** This process removes the dirt and any blemishes from the wood, restoring it to its original golden-brown. It is like adding a cup of bleach to your whites.

There are a number of two-part cleaning/bleaching solutions on the market. Below I have listed two that work best for me. (For more on cleaning and bleaching, see Chapter 4, Teak Tips.)

1) Teka: This product is **very strong** and great to use on teak that has been neglected for a long time. Dilute with water if teak is in good shape.

Follow the directions on the back of the manufacturer's container and the advice listed below:

a) Soap down any areas TEKA may run across before applying solutions.

b) Wear gloves and shoes. TEKA will do to your body what it does to the wood.

c) **TEKA will ruin aluminum.**

d) Be careful where you walk with TEKA on your shoes. I can recall an interior with beautiful, light-blue carpet that had permanent TEKA-brown footprints across it.

e) **Always** have two people working with TEKA. One person to scrub and one to keep the chemicals wet and off surrounding surfaces.

f) **Do not** let any part of TEKA dry out. Keep a fine mist of water going over the area at all times.

g) Buy more than enough solution to get the job done. Running out of one part or the other would be sentencing your wood to a life of discoloration.

h) Be sure wood is dry before sanding. See Sanding After Cleaning/Bleaching below.

2) TSP (Trisodium Phosphate) And Oxalic Acid: This method is not as potent as TEKA and will leave your wood a silvery-brown rather than the golden-brown of TEKA. This duo has been around for many years and can be found in most any hardware store. (Because Trisodium Phosphate is not biodegradable, I urge you to try using a biodegradable soap and lots of elbow grease first.)

Let wood dry completely, then follow the Sanding After Cleaning/Bleaching as described next.

Sanding After Cleaning/Bleaching

Wood feels like it has been raped after a good cleaning and bleaching. Shock is shown through protruding grain standing on end.

To make the wood right again, the hard grain must be sanded away. Start with #80-grit sandpaper, then #120 and end with a fine paper such as #220-grit. When you have obtained a super-smooth, level finish, see Clearing the Decks next.

Clearing the Decks

The only thing left to do at this stage is to clear the decks and make way for the varnish!

Take an abrasive pad, such as a 3-M Scotch-Brite pad, and some water and scrub down the sanded surface. Using the abrasive pad ensures cleanliness and also adds an extra "tooth" to the surface.

While you are washing down your surfaces, pay close attention to what they look like wet. Are the yellow-air pockets and bandaged areas disappearing when wet? If not, they won't when varnished either. This is your last chance to fix those areas.

After you are sure the surface is clean, hose off surrounding areas. You don't want any dust around that might get stirred up later and land in your varnish, you have worked too hard for that to happen.

Some expert varnisher's use a vacuum to clean up. This is a good method if you are in an area where the water wouldn't dry and it would put a kink in your progress.

After your surface is clean, take a break. When you get back, the surface should be clean and dry.

If you have been meticulous in preparing the surfaces, you will be pleased with the results.

Varnishing Checklist
    [ ]   Ideal Weather Conditions
    [ ]   Drop Cloth
    [ ]   Tack Rag
    [ ]   Masking Tape
    [ ]   Proper Thinner to Conform to Weather
    [ ]   Varnish
    [ ]   Brushes
    [ ]   Clean Containers
    [ ]   Clean Cotton Rags
    [ ]   Sharp Razor Blad/Pin
    [ ]   Stick-to-itiveness

To Mask or Not to Mask?

I know a few professional varnishers who can really cut a fine line with their brushes and do not need to use masking tape on their surfaces.

But I recommend masking be done. Using masking tape, tape off the bottom side where the teak meets the gel coat or paint. It is not really necessary to tape off the top side because the varnish will not run up.

Are Your Rags Good Enough?

Prevent all rags from touching a prepared surface unless you know where they have been.

For example, if a rag was used for dusting the interior, or waxing the topsides, it will be contaminated with traces of oil and wax. These substances will prevent the varnish from sticking to the surface.

Buying Brushes

Purchase either a polyfoam disposable brush, or a top of the line brand name such as **Badger**. The cheaper bristle brushes tend to shed themselves in wet varnish, which does not make for a good time.

Preparing Brushes

If you are using a polyfoam brush, check it for unwanted hitchhikers and simply whisk them away. However, if you are going to be using a bristle brush, submerge the bristles in thinner and spin the handle between your palms and fingers. Do this in a container so that the thinner and whatever is clinging to it does not go all over the boat. Do this procedure two or three times.

Quit Eyeballing That Can!

If you have the urge to varnish out of the manufacturer's can, don't. Doing so will only contaminate the varnish. Use paper buckets which can be found in any marine hardware store, although be cautious. After a few hours of use, they tend to soften around the bottom and become moist. At that time, if you set the bucket down, it will leave a ring of varnish.

Better yet, use clean, empty soup cans or the like, which will accommodate your brush size. **Stay away from glass jars of any kind.** Breaking one on the boat or dock could be quite dangerous.

Pour just enough varnish in the container to get you from point A to point B. This will keep the varnish clean and prevent needless waste.

Thinning Varnish to Conform to the Weather

Think of the weather and varnish in terms of a one-sided marriage. The weather is set in her ways and unwilling to change. The varnish must conform to her moods if the marriage is going to work.

When needed, we help the varnish agree with his partner by adding a particular thinner to it. Most marine paint manufacturers produce slow and fast thinners for different brushing and weather conditions.

For example, **Z-Spar** makes numbered thinners. The higher the number, the slower the thinner. The lower the number, the faster the thinner.

In summer months, when temperatures are warmer, you will want to use a higher numbered thinner (T-11) to slow down the varnish's drying time. If you don't, it will dry too fast, not flow properly, and lap marks will appear.

In winter months when temperatures are cooler, use a lower numbered thinner (T-8). This thinner will set the varnish off quick and get it well on its way to drying before you lose the best part of the day.

How Much Thinner?

Because you want the first coat of varnish to penetrate deep into the wood, the formula should be one-quarter thinner to three-quarters varnish.

For additional coats, the varnish should be the same consistency as when if **first** came out of the manufacturer's can. When you notice it thickening, or your brush dragging, add about a teaspoon of thinner and stir gently.

Filling Your Brush

1) Polyfoam: Submerge the sponge halfway into the varnish. It will fill quickly. On the count of three, pull the brush out.

2) Bristle Brush: Dip the bristles one-third to one-half their length into the varnish. Any excess should be eliminated by tapping the bristles against the side of the container. Do not drag them across the top. Doing so ruins their natural shape.

Flow a Coat

Stop where you are! Before you flow that coat, take a tack rag and go over the prepared surfaces. Varnish should *flow* across a prepared surface like molasses on a sheet of glass. With this in mind, flow on about four inches of varnish using light, even strokes in all directions to ensure absorption into the pores. End with strokes going in one direction with the

Working into the wet will be your best bet.

grain. Do not overwork the varnish. The less you brush, the better the results.

Start again a few inches away from the wet patch and work back toward it. You should always be pulling your brush into the wet varnish, not away from it. Continue in this manner. (See illustration, page 63).

Do not put a lot of pressure on the brush. You want the brush to barely touch the surface you are varnishing. The varnish should separate the brush from the surface.

If you find the brush dragging, the varnish is too thick or you are not using enough of it. If the varnish drips, you are either using too much, or it is too thin.

If your brush is becoming sticky, your hands probably are too. Take a minute and clean up. This will prevent the varnish from running down your arm and you will feel better after a break.

Flying Objects

If you notice a bug take a nose dive into your wet varnish, ignore it. Saving its life is not worth ruining your finish.

When the varnish dries, brush away what remains of the unfortunate bug with a soft cotton rag. Its little paw prints will barely be noticeable. This also goes for dust particles and the like.

If the problem is an innocent bystander's hand print, you may as well have them date it and then throw them into the bay.

Drying Time Between Coats

There is no set time because all areas differ. What dries on the west coast in a day may take three on the east coast.

The best thing to do is test the varnish in an inconspicuous area with your fingernail. If some comes off, it is not cured enough.

How Many Coats?

From the list below, find the surface preparation method you performed and apply the essential coats recommended.

Method	Coats
#220-Grit method	1
#60-grit Knock-Down	3
Varnish Stripping	6

After these vital coats are applied, flow on a coat every three months. **Do not wait until your varnish starts looking diseased!**

However, if you keep your varnish covered (which is the wise thing to do) and well maintained, you can go as long as a year without adding a coat. See Maintaining Varnish: Enemy Overboard in Chapter 2.

Storing Varnish

Do not pour used varnish back into the manufacturer's can! Discard properly. And I do not mean into the harbor. That may sound like common sense but you would be surprised.

After varnish has been opened, its nature is to form a skin over the top. To eliminate this problem, seal the lid tight so no air can get in and store the can upside down. Next time you use the varnish, the skin will be on the bottom.

Diseased Varnish

Before you bring the boat doctor down to see your sick varnish, see if you can diagnose the problem yourself by using the list below.

Black Spots. Looks like the varnish has dark patches of wood warts. They are caused by dirt or mildew penetrating the varnish and soiling the underlying wood.

Blistering. Varnish seems to have an acne problem. This condition may be due to moisture trapped beneath the varnish or a foreign substance coming from the inside out.

Brushmarks. You would think Picasso had been there. These marks are left by working the varnish too much, or the varnish skimming before it has a chance to flow out.

Keeping your varnish on a healthy maintenance program will prevent the aches, pains and expense brought on by the boat doctor.

Cracking. Like dry skin it begins to crack open. This condition is due to the varnish being thick, old, and weathered.

Curtains. This varnish looks like the person who lost all the weight but not the flab. Too much varnish was used or it was too thick.

Flat. Varnish with anemia causing it to lack its full luster. This is what happens when temperatures drop before the varnish has a chance to skim.

Gatoring. Remember Aunt Ruth's alligator bag? This condition is usually brought on by the puddling of thick varnish.

Grittiness. Looks like the non-skid on the deck of a boat. Using dirty methods and brushes cause this effect.

Holidays. Small (hopefully) areas missed in the varnished surface that remind the perfectionists that even they are not beyond error.

Nicks and Dings. Battle wounds that can be easily mended. These tragedies usually occur on the weekends when you invite your non-boating friend, Mr. Landlubber, for a Sunday bay cruise. In his excitement, he slams his six-pack down on your varnished caprail.

Runs. Looks like the varnish has shed a tear here and there. The misfortune is due to applying too much varnish at one time, not brushing it out, and sloppy work habits.

Spidery Lines. The varnish looks like a spider "webbed" all over it. Caused by over exposure to the weather.

Yellow-Air-Pockets. Imprisoned air bubbles that held their breath so long their little faces turned yellow. These are caused by some type of trauma to the varnished surface.

Your Rights

You have the right-of-way when it comes to a wet varnished surface. If you are varnishing on a boat and the guy next to you decides he wants to do some sanding, you have the right to tell him to stop. Dust particles may end up in your wet varnish. If he is a jerk and sands anyway, he is responsible for any damage he may have caused.

I am reminded of a summer when Bill Beck and I were varnishing on two separate boats. Some guys in the boatyard next to us started grinding away with their sanders. Because we were downwind, the dust particles settled nicely into our fresh varnish.

Bill told them to stop. I remember thinking, that big boatyard wasn't going to stop production for a pair of insignificant boat maintainers. But, to my surprise, they did.

Hiring a Professional

The best advice I can give in looking for a professional is to ask a neighboring boat owner, or the manager of your favorite marine hardware store. Word of mouth is, most often, great advertisement.

I know of a boat owner that really got stung because he didn't do his homework before hiring a "here in the summer, gone in the winter," young person.

Fly-by-night, told the boat owner that he needed to be paid half the amount being charged before he could start the job. In blind faith, the boat owner gave him about five-hundred dollars.

The boat was never touched.

Cover It Up!

Whether you have just read this chapter, or have already physically experienced the joys and pains of varnishing, you are aware of the time and money involved in obtaining a quality finish.

Knowing this, why wouldn't you cover it up? You would not let a sea gull dump on your Waterford crystal would you?

The Ten Commandments of Varnishing

1) Check The Weather Forecast

2) Mother Nature Has The Final Say

3) Do Not Get Caught With Your Varnish Down

4) Pay Close Attention To Details

5) Preparation Is 99% Of The Finished Product

6) Practice Clean Work Habits

7) Thin Varnish To Conform To The Weather

8) Always Layoff Into The Wet

9) Flow A Coat Before Varnish Looks Diseased

10) Cover It Up

6

COMPOUNDING AND WAXING GEL COAT

Sher's definition of compounding and waxing: *"An endless, grueling game called 'Shine and Shield'. The object of the game is to keep the sun's destructive clutches from making chalk out of the gel coat."*

Rest assured, if you are ignoring your boat's gel coat, the sun is reducing it to a powder.

Most often, boat owner's do not realize they have been neglecting their gel coat until after a relaxing harbor cruise. As they are getting off their boat, they look down at their most cherished boating outfit and realize there is more gel coat on their clothes than on the boat.

Do not be a gel coat abuser. It is not wise to ignore 20 thousandths of an inch coat of resin whose only purpose in life is to keep your boat afloat. Once it is gone, it is gone for good.

That Magical Fiberglass Armor

Because fiberglass cannot withstand the pressures of a harsh marine environment, and cosmetically it would send any would-be boat owner screaming out the doors headed toward the wooden boat factory, it is protected by a coat of armor that is both strong and fine to look at: gel coat.

Gel coat is a hard, but flexible, pigmented resin. It will always take care of your fiberglass as long as you take care of it by keeping it clean and waxed.

Compounding

Whether gel coat is in good shape or bad, it must always be compounded before it is waxed. The compound cleans away any dead materials and fills in small scratches, thus making the gel coat shine. (Compound makes the gel coat shine, not the wax.)

If you do not compound the gel coat before you wax it, the boat may end up like the poor fellows below.

A friend of mine, Chuck Reed, whose forte is compounding and waxing fiberglass boats, told me of a time he gave a bid on a job but had some young kid under bid him about two-thousand dollars. (The boat was a mess.)

In what Chuck and his crew would have done in two weeks, the young hustler had done in a day.

The boat looked good for about a week. But at the end of the seventh day, the gel coat was dull again with huge flat streaks going through it where the oxidation, that should have been taken off in the first place, was bleeding through the wax.

Unfortunately, the boat owner who thought he was getting a deal, got ripped off instead. All the kid did was saturate the oxidation with some wax which made the gel coat look wet for a very short time. You could get the same effect by putting water on a sanded surface. It looks great when it is wet, but when it dries it looks the same, if not worse.

I have seen different methods used around the harbor and Mr. Hustlers' is not one I recommend.

First of all, using the descriptions below, determine to what degree the surface of the gel coat has deteriorated, if at all. Keep in mind that the worse it is, the harsher your products must be to clean it up.

(Because the sun will make the job more miserable than it already is, move the boat into some shade. If moving it is not possible, get an early start.)

"Pristine": Since day one, this gel coat has been kept cleaned and waxed on a regular basis. This has kept the sun from starting its deterioration process.

The answer is simple: using soft cotton rags on gel coat that is only twenty-thousandths of an inch thick will ensure longer life than taking a harsh polishing machine to it.

Because this gel coat is in such good shape, it is only necessary to use a fiberglass cleaner/wax on it. (Sea Power puts out an excellent cleaner/wax.)

The cleaner/wax contains a fine rubbing compound to clean the surface and a thin coat of wax to seal it. Apply the substance to the surface using a soft cotton rag and take it off in the same fashion. Gel coat in this good of shape has never known trauma. Do not start by taking a machine to it.

"Just a hint": This is the gel coat that does not get any attention until it shows signs of deterioration. The boat owner will wait until he sees a chalk-like substance develop over the resin. And waiting for the "hint" only means he is going to be taking off more of the gel coat.

To clean up this gel coat, use a paste fiberglass rubbing coumpound. (Boat Armour and Dupont make a great product.) These types of compounds are "gritty" and will remove the dead pigment to get to some new gel coat. Some professionals mix a cleaner/wax with the compound for moisture, which makes the substance easier to work with.

Working the compound into the gel coat can be done one of two ways: You can use a white Scotch-Brite pad by 3M, which comes attached to a handle or use a power polisher with a nylon buffing pad.

If you are going to be using a machine, be very careful. Keep in mind that a layer of gel coat is very thin and a machine removes a lot of gel coat at one time and could go right through to the fiberglass. It also leaves tiny swirl marks if not properly handled.

When compounding is done, apply a hard paste fiberglass wax. (See Waxing on the following pages.)

"Used-to-be gel coat": The only thing that remains of this gel coat is chalk. It should be removed so it can be on its way to gel coat heaven.

Usually removing gel coat that is this bad takes an extreme measure such as wet and dry sanding. It can only work once because so much gel coat is being removed. Although, if a shiny surface can be obtained and with proper maintenance, it could last for a few more years.   Otherwise, the surface will have to be painted.

Consult a professional.

Waxing

After compounding, the gel coat is left unprotected and up for grabs. Applying wax to the gel coat is like appointing its very own bodyguard.

Use a hard paste fiberglass wax. Do not use an automobile wax. The car wax chemists sitting down in their labs are not thinking about designing a wax for a boat.

Most fiberglass waxes contain three essential ingredients: silicones, carnuaba, and an ultra violet screen.

Apply and take off the wax by hand using soft cotton rags. (I just do not believe in using machines unless you need to remove a thin layer of gel coat. Otherwise, they are not very nice to a boat's surface.)

How Many Coats of Wax?

The key is not how many coats of wax you put on at one time, rather how often you compound and wax.

Most fiberglass waxes stick to the surface, not to themselves. So if you apply that extra coat, it may fill in where the first did not, but it won't give extra protection.

How Often?

Some boat owners think just because the gel coat is shiny it does not need to be cleaned or waxed. Not true. The wax may still be worn off.

That's why it is very important that you have some type of schedule set up for your boat. I recommend compounding and waxing four times a year. However, in some areas, where the ultra violet rays may not be as strong, like in some northern latitudes or in your garage, you may not need to compound and wax as often. It is best, depending upon where your boat is stored, to use your better judgement.

Remember: Once the sun breaks down the wax, it will do the same to the gel coat.

Keep Her Clean

The more clean you keep the gel coat, the longer it is going to last. (See Chapter 2, Wash Downs). Also, adding a liquid wash/wax to your wash down water will help preserve the wax.

In Search of the Quick Fix

I have to admit, maintaining gel coat can sometimes be a time consuming job not meant for man or beast. But for heaven's sake, do not think you are doing yourself a favor by pouring acrylic floor polish all over her. That acrylic shine will cost you more than if you would have done it right in the first place.

Do not get me wrong. It looks great when you first pour it on and you will think you found the answer to a boat maintenance prayer. But, after a year, your quick fix prayer turns into a never fix nightmare.

After the sun has had some time to work on the acrylic polish, it turns it into the ugliest brown that does not come off easily. I would rather be the boat owner that let my gel coat go, than the one stuck with a permanent cast of gloom over his boat.

You Expecting a Miracle, Mister?

If you have let your gel coat go without any preventative maintenance, you can be sure it is going to cost you when you want it restored. The result is either physically abusing your own body, or monetarily assaulting your wallet. Preventative maintenance is cheaper and does not hurt as much as paying for a miracle.

7

RUNNING AND
STANDING RIGGING

Sher's definition of a finely tuned rig: *"One that stands proud without fear of falling, and runs gracefully through the water like a song free of limitations."*

When it comes to maintaining the rig and its counterparts, it goes without saying that a sailboat owner has greater responsibilities than those of a powerboat owner. However, for such things as lifelines, turnbuckles and stanchions, the obligations are shared by both.

Neglect is a poor excuse for a shroud that gives way under a full sail, or for lifelines that collapse under a person's full body weight.

A Ticket Aloft

If the lack of transportation has been the only reason you have not been up to inspect the top of your mast, you have probably never heard of the "bosun's chair."

The bosun's chair has been the sailor's ticket to the top for years. It can be found in most marine hardware stores and is a **must** investment that will easily pay its own way.

When purchasing a bosun's chair, make sure it has the following features: 1) made of canvas; 2) a wooden seat sewn into the cloth; 3) plenty of pockets for tools; 4) a safety belt. (Modernization has really done us a favor in terms of safety, comfort, and convenience when you think back to when sailors simply went aloft on a piece of wood and some rope.)

There is safety in numbers. Never go aloft alone.

Remember the old saying, "There is safety in numbers?" Well, if it has never applied to any aspect of your life, it does now. Never go aloft alone. Have at least one other person there to crank you up the mast and be there in case you need him. (Can you imagine spending the night fifty feet up in the air clinging for your life to a mast? Me either.)

Here is a list of some steadfast advice to follow when preparing for and going aloft:

1) You must trust that the gear pulling you up the mast will not fail. If you don't, don't use it.

2) Do not rely solely on the shackle that connects the bosun's chair to the halyard to hold all your weight. Devise a safety line of some sort, like the one shown in the illustration, so you have a back-up in case of an emergency.

3) The safest halyard to go up on is an *internal halyard*, which runs inside the mast and over a sheave. I do not recommend going up on blocks which are attached to a tang outside the mast because there is no way to secure that system.

4) Do not go up on a spinnaker halyard.

5) Do not go aloft on a windy day unless you are into slamming against stays, shrouds, and the mast.

6) Tie any tools to the chair with rope long enough that you can still use them. This will prevent you from dropping them on the deck or on your buddy's head below.

7) As you are being cranked aloft, keep both hands on the mast at all times.

Standing Rigging

The *standing rigging* on a sailboat is all the rigging that holds up the mast: shrouds, hold the mast from port to starboard; stays, steady the mast from forward and aft; swaged terminal ends; turnbuckles; speaders; chainplates; and (of course), the mast.

Shrouds and Stays. For the most part, dirty shrouds and stays will not fail. But, they could cause

DON'T   **DO**

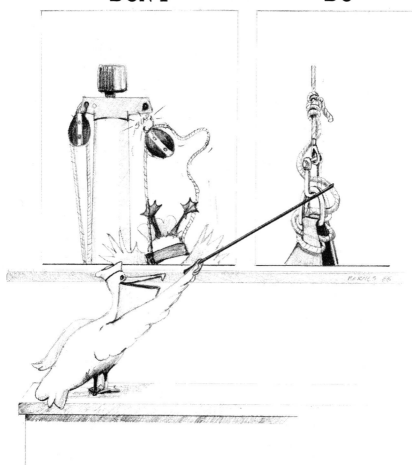

When going aloft, DO attach a safety line from the bosun's chair to the halyard and DO NOT go up on an external halyard.

79

damage to other parts of the boat like the decking and sails.

For example, let us take the sails that are left hanked to a dirty headstay. Dew spirals down the stay picking up the hitchhiking dirt for a traveling companion. By the time this pair hits the sails, they have turned into one big mess leaving dirty black streaks in the folds of the sails.

Also, moisture and dirt that constantly drip from shrouds and stays are the cause of those impossible to remove rust stains often found on the decking.

There are three ways to clean shrouds and stays:

1) Take a hose, a Scotch-Brite pad, and some rags aloft with you. Scrub the wiring with the pad and rinse off with fresh water. Swing fore and aft working your way down. Wipe the mast off as you go.

2) If you prefer not to take the hose up, stand on the deck and squirt the rigging so you get most of the dirt off. Then, take a bucket of fresh water, a Scotch-Brite pad, and some rags and do as stated in number 1.

3) If you are hauling out the boat, the shrouds and stays can easily be cleaned on land.

As you are cleaning, you should be inspecting the wiring also. If you notice any broken wires, this is usually a sign that they need to be replaced. However, for the time being, they can be taped so they cannot put any holes in the sails or in your body.

Swaged Fittings. Unlike some fittings that can be attached by hand, like the Norseman and Sta-lok types, the swaged fittings (which are most common) are secured by using a swedging machine. The machine literally marries the wire rope to the turnbuckles together forever unless, through constant neglect, they part.

These fittings should be inspected for hairline cracks and corrosion. If signs occur, it means something is going on inside the hardware that should not be.

Because moisture and impurities from the stainless steel cause wear, a periodic dose of WD-40 (or the like) will help eliminate the problem.

Turnbuckles. Turnbuckles are used to apply tension to the rigging. If tightening the turnbuckles does not take up the slack in the rigging, check shrouds and stays from the mast to the chainplates.

Turnbuckles must be turned every so often or they will freeze up in one position and be useless. Lube with WD-40.

If you have turnbuckle boots or tape over the turnbuckles, do not let this stop you from inspecting the hardware. Believe it or not, the turnbuckles and their counterparts will survive if you do not cover them. They look better too.

Chainplates. Inspect chainplates and make sure they are secured to the boat. If there is a problem, call a professional.

Masts. Whether aluminum or wood, the mast should be kept clean and inspected regularly. Check the fasteners and make sure they are doing what they should be. Check for cracks, something coming apart, rust and corrosion.

The sheave(s) at the top of the mast should spin freely and the surface should be smooth and free from defects that may damage the halyard. Spray with WD-40.

A wooden mast should be checked for dry rot, especially around fittings that attract moisture.

If there are any major repairs to be done, you will stay younger if the mast is taken down and repaired on dry land.

Running Rigging

Running rigging is best defined as anything that moves to run the sails: halyards, sheets, winches and blocks. All should be kept healthy enough to set and trim the sails.

Halyards. A *halyard* is the line that pulls the sails up and down. Because this line takes more strain than the others, it must be checked periodically

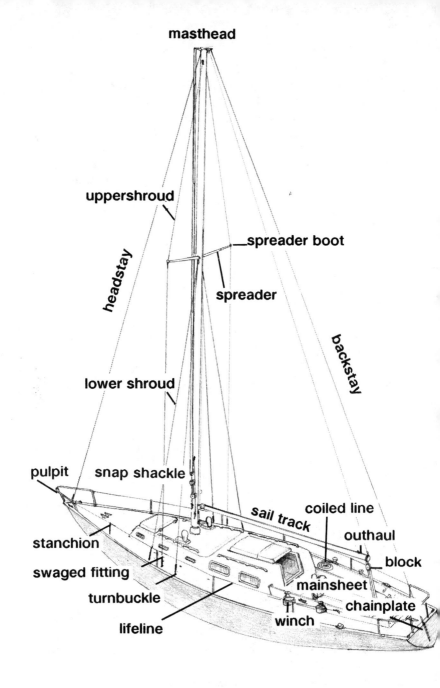

Running and standing rigging.

for chafe. The best way to inspect it is to remove it from the mast by hand.

Sheets. *Sheets* adjust the sails. There are two different ways to clean sheets. One, put sheets in a bucket of fresh water and mild detergent and stomp on them like grapes, then rinse with plenty of fresh water; or two, put sheets in a pillowcase, or net bag, and wash in the washing machine with a mild detergent. Let them air dry. Do not put them in the dryer.

Winches. These hardworking devices deserve some tender-loving-care every once in a while, at least annually.

Disassemble and soak parts in a bucket of diesel fuel or paint thinner. After soaking, grease parts and reassemble. Watch out for the small parts and the ones that jump out at you. It is a good idea to cover scuppers so the little parts cannot abandon ship.

If you do not feel comfortable disassembling a winch, try to get a hold of an owner's manual or call a professional.

Blocks. Keep clean with fresh water and lubricate bearings with WD-40.

Take Your Hands Off My Lifeline

The most common reason lifelines and stanchions become loose is due to the fact that the eager beaver person waiting anxiously on the dock to help you into your slip grabs hold of them and pulls with all his might in an heroic effort to help you.

Every time someone pulls on this lifesaving system, it lessens the chance that a life might be saved when thrown up against it.

If the stanchions are loose, unbolt them from the decking, clean out the old coumpound, and fill in with new. Do this not only for safety, but also for prevention of leaks.

8

SAILS AND COVERS

Sher's definition of maintaining sails and covers: *"Keeping engines composed of wind from 'blowing-out', and safekeepers made of canvas from going to the scrap pile."*

Are you using and abusing your boats sails and covers? Do you find that the only time you pay attention to their existence is when you need them to power or protect your boat?

If you answered "yes" to the above questions, this is what you have to look forward to (if you are not already): Cosmetic degeneration every time you hoist dirty sails and/or lay shoddy looking covers; early breakdown of materials due to neglect; and forking out more money for items that would have lasted two to three times longer had they been properly maintained.

These inescapable facts remind me of a time I was sitting in my beach chair watching the boats go in and out of Dana Point Harbor. (One of my favorite pastimes is searching for cosmetic perfection in boats). I caught sight of a 38' Ericson which was in such perfect cosmetic condition that it sparkled in the sun. I was delighted to watch it motor by me, until the sails were hoisted. They were so filthy, they made the boat look the same. I couldn't understand the reasoning behind it.

Put the attitude that sails and covers don't need preventative maintenance out with next weeks trash pick-up. Add them to your maintenance schedule and enjoy enhancing the looks of your boat, doubling

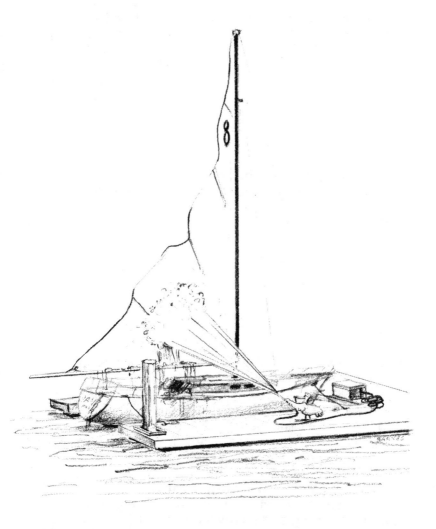

After spending time out at sea, rinse the sails thoroughly with plenty of fresh water. Otherwise, the salt molecules will make confetti out of the insides of the sail cloth.

their lifetime and spending your money in Mexico instead of at the sailmakers or canvas shop.

Maintaining Sails

There are many different types of sailcloth on the market today: Dacron, which is most widely used; Terylene; Kevlar; Mylar; and Nylon. But, unfortunately, choosing between one or the other has nothing to do with one holding up better than the other.

They are all engines of wind made out of a different cloth but are the same in that they all battle the same destructive forces: chafing, stretching, creases and folds, moisture, dirt, mildew, salt and over exposure to sunlight.

Sails do not require too much attention to keep them safe from the above demons. However, the wrong kind of care could be detrimental to them.

Educate yourself about the sailcloth on your boat. And always handle it delicately. If you do, your sails will pay their own way and bring you many hours of pure pleasure as they propel you away from reality.

Routine Rinsing. Whether racing or just cruising, the combination of ocean, sun, and excitement can sometimes deplete one of so much energy, that rinsing the salt out of the sails once back into port is the last thing one wants to do. But, if one was to look at a salt molecule under a microscope, it just might recharge one's batteries.

Unbeknownst to the average naked eye are the sharp ragged edges of a salt crystal. Magnified, one salt molecule looks like a snowflake with razor-sharp edges. When thousands of these snaggle-toothed varmints are left in the sails, they literally enjoy making confetti out of the inside of the sailcloth.

Unless you like the idea of having the inside of your sails ripped to shreds, rinse them out with plenty of fresh water after returning from a trip out at sea. Maximize rinsing and let dry thoroughly before stowing.

Just in case I have not convinced you yet, if you do not rinse the salt out of your sails, one day instead of experiencing some time-out while out at sea, you may have a "blow-out" instead.

Wash sails on a clean, non-abrasive surface and
hang to dry properly.

A *blow-out* is when the sails have weakened so much due to neglect (the stitching is usually the first to go) that they burst open like a worn tire on a car. And, like a flat tire, you will go nowhere with a blown-out sail. Unless you carry a spare!

Washing. This section concerns sailcloth made of Dracon. I recommend dyed sails be cleaned by a professional who specializes in them.

Sails should be taken off the boat for a thorough scrubbing at least once a season and always before stowing away for the winter.

For best results, sails should be spread flat on a clean non-abrasive surface. Scrubbing on an abrasive surface, such as asphalt, will abrade the fibers. Unfortunately, if your boat is any bigger than a trailerboat or day sailer, you practically need a football field made of concrete to do the job. Do not wash your sails on a lawn. Doing so can cause permanent grass stains.

Scrub the sails with a soft bristle brush, using a mild non-alkaline detergent, such as Woolite or Ivory. Alkaline can make some sailcloths more sensitive to ultra violet rays which weaken the fibers. Weak fibers attract more dirt.

Because scrubbing can breakdown the resins in the cloth, only scrub in one area for about 20 seconds.

Stains. Instant removal of a substance which will stain the sailcloth will prevent future heartache. If, however, you do encounter a stain or two during your washing procedure, ask yourself if the stain would be better left alone rather than risking the integrity of the sailcloth?

If you want to give it a go, here is my advice for the most common stains found in Dacron sailcloth:

Mildew: First, remove the surface mildew using a stiff, dry, bristle brush. Make a solution of bleach and fresh water (one part bleach to twenty parts fresh water). Work the solution into the stained area using your stiff bristle brush, start from the center of the stain and work outward. If you do not notice a reaction, try soaking the area in the solution for two to three hours. Afterward, rinse with plenty of fresh water.

Grease and Oil: Rub over the stain with a stain remover which contains *trichlorocthane*, such as Renuzit or Energine. Rinse thoroughly with fresh water.

Rust Stains: Soak the stained section of the sail in a solution of oxalic acid and fresh water (one part oxalic acid to ten parts fresh water). Rinse with fresh water.

Hosing Off and Drying. After washing, sails should be hung as if from a clothesline so they can be rinsed thoroughly and dried naturally. Be sure to hang the sails by the luft so that their weight is supported rather than stretched. (See the illustration on page 87.)

When rinsing, use five times more water than you feel is necessary. You want to be sure all traces of detergent are out of the sails. To combat against mildew, let dry completely before stowing.

Also, while the sails are hanging around it is a great time to get a pen and paper and inspect them for the following: loose stitching, chafing, unusual wear, and any tears or holes.

If any repairs are needed, take them to your local sail loft to have them fixed. This way they will be ready to go the next time you are.

Stowing. There are four things to remember when stowing your sails:

1) Be sure they are clean and dry.
2) Be sure they are properly "flaked". (See the illustration page 90.)
3) Be sure they are kept covered -- always.
4) Do not ignore repairs when they are minor. Ignored minor repairs turn into haunting major ones.

Never cram sails into their bags. Doing so will cause the sails to develop creases and folds which reduce their effectiveness. And **No**, you cannot iron them like a piece of clothing. (See page 91.)

Your sails will be around a lot longer if they are flaked properly before stowing.

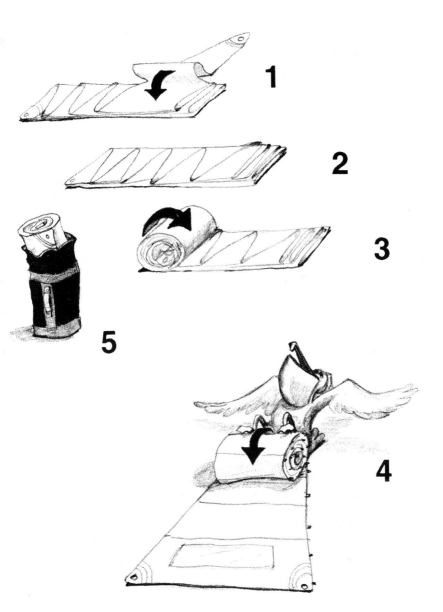

Fold sails correctly before putting them into their sail bag. Cramming them only causes creases which reduces their effectiveness.

Dirty Rigging. . . Clean Sails?

It may be a good idea to incorporate cleaning the rigging with washing your sails. It could be quite disheartening to watch your snowy-white sails lay up against dirty, black shrouds. (See Chapter 7, Running and Standing Rigging.)

Protecting Canvas Safekeepers

I knew of a boat owner who thought the easiest way to wash his covers was to take them to the neighborhood laundromat and wash them in the machines there.

After such a rugged experience, the covers had shrunk so much that the only boat they might have fit was Barbie and Kens'.

It is okay if you want to put small covers (winch, binnacle or compass) into the washer under delicate cycle. But do not dry them in the dryer! Hang them so they can air dry.

Wash covers as you would a sail. Spread them out on a clean, non-abrasive surface and scrub with a brush and mild detergent. Hang, rinse thoroughly with fresh water, and let air dry.

Once a month vacuum covers to get rid of dust.

If the covers are brand new, or in good condition, treat them with a fabric protector such as Scotchgard. The fabric is still allowed to breath while whatever lands on them will adhere to the resistor rather than the fabric. By the way, did you know that the acids in bird guano bleach canvas?

Having your covers treated will make maintaining them 100% easier. They will last longer and they won't have bleached out imprints of bird droppings on them.

Pick Up and Deliver

Did you know that in some areas of the country there are companies who will pick up dirty sails and covers, wash and dry them and return them to the customer in a neat clean package? I didn't either until just recently.

In researching information for this chapter I learned of a company in Newport Beach, California, called *Aqua Marine*, who was more than generous in providing me with additional infomation on how to care for sails and covers.

If you are unable to wash your own sails and covers, I highly recommend utilizing a company such as *Aqua Marine*. I know that time and space to lay out the sails are major factors that limit the boat owner from doing it himself. But these are not problems for those professionals who are in the business of preserving the life of your sails and covers.

9

OH YEAH. . .
THE BILGE

Sher's definition of a clean, religiously inspected bilge: *"Peace of mind knowing that you won't be sharing below deck with horrendous odors or an unexpected high tide."*

If the bilge on a boat is overlooked when it comes to maintenance, it is usually for one or all of these reasons: One, it has a stink-hole reputation and nobody wants to go near it; two, it is camoflaged by floorboards and nobody knows it exists; or three, there is no access to it.

However, an ignored bilge has ways of getting its owners' attention. For example, one bilge introduced itself to its owner by giving off rotten odors that were so bad, his guests were green with seasickness. The bilge was telling the boat owner that the head pipe had sprung a leak.

Another bilge made its existence known to the boat owner because of a shower through hull clamp had been allowed to rust away. One morning the boat owner came down to the dock to find his boat under five feet of water.

A bilge should not have to put its owner through such distressing experiences as the ones mentioned above to get some attention. Keep in mind that a bilge is only a "stink-hole" because it is not clean. It is only camoflaged because the owner keeps it that way. If there is no access to it, make one.

There is no excuse for unpleasant smells or boats that list, especially because most bilges can be self-

Do not let your first introduction to your bilge be a wet one.

cleaning. It does not take much effort to hold a flashlight and open your eyes.

Cleaning the Bilge
The two most important reasons to keep the bilge clean is to prevent bacteria growth, and to keep bad odors from forming.

Marine hardware stores sell a bilge cleaner which works well but can be costly. I have found that using liquid Tide is much cheaper and it does a great job. It contains no phosphorus, is biodegradable, cuts grease and dirt, and to top it off, has a wonderful clean smell.

Some boats take in more water than others. If the boat you are concerned with usually has water in its bilge, add the liquid Tide, and let the rock and roll of the boat do the cleaning for you. (Be sure you know that the water you are taking on is not coming from a leaking through hull fitting or pipe.)

Do not allow water to remain in the bilge for prolonged periods of time. It may cause rust, mildew and peeling paint. Besides, IT STINKS!

Limber Holes. These are ducts located in the bilge which allow water to pass through them and flow to the lowest point of the bilge where it will be pumped out either manually or automatically.

It is essential that these ducts be kept clear of residue which may block the passage of water. Otherwise, you will have a fine mess to clean up.

Engine Oil Drips. Hopefully, before someone installed the engine(s) in your boat, they were nice enough to put down an oil drip pan first. If not, any oil dripping from the engine goes into the bilge instead of the pan.

Whether you are changing the oil, cleaning oil from a drip pan, or chasing oil leaks down the bilge, there are two items that work the best in absorbing the oil: feminine napkins and disposable diapers. Use whichever one you are the least embarrassed to purchase and the one easiest to explain to curious neighbors!

Inspecting the Bilge

A bilge, and its surroundings, should be inspected once a month with the aid of a flashlight. Here is a list of things which should pass an honest visual inspection:

1) Unusual amounts of water should be traced to the source of leakage.
2) Check float arm on electric bilge pump. Lift it up and make sure it comes on.
3) Check through hull openings and fittings. Make sure fittings are secure and in good shape. I have heard horror stories of boats sinking just because a through hull fitting came loose.
4) Seacocks should be opened and closed to insure they are working properly.
5) Look for corrosion everywhere and check for any unusual growth.
6) Check pipes, hoses, and clamps
7) If the boat is wooden, check for wood rot.
8) Check limber holes.

Steam Cleaning

Normally, most grease and dirt can be removed with some detergent and elbow grease. However, if you are not willing to succumb to that method, steam cleaning is an alternative.

Keep in mind that steam cleaning is a harsh method that can cause paint to peel, especially on wood.

I recommend you do not try it yourself. Call a professional, ask them questions, and call their references.

Do Not Dump In the Bay!

Discharging waste into a harbor is something a child might do because he didn't know any better. Threats are things we use to try to get the child from polluting the bay any further, like: Putting dye in the boat's holding tank so when there is a discharge we know where it is coming from; or marking boats that have no holding tank in order to monitor them.

Using pumpouts to dispose of waste is something mature, caring adults do. Adult's who do not feel there are enough pumpouts to service the whole harbor, should go to public city council meetings and voice their opinions.

An adult boat owner loves the ocean and realizes polluting it is no act of affection but one of comtempt or carelessness. Even a child knows comtempt or apathy can be harmful. We all need to act as adults. It is too important not to care.

10

INTERIORS

Sher's definition of a boat's interior: *"A buoyant feeling of being home."*

Unlike the exterior that is always fighting harmful elements, an interior's only battle is with its owner.

We were asked to go down to Dana Point Harbor and clean a 42' Westsail. The outside of the boat was not too bad, but when we opened the hatch and looked inside, our first reactions were to close the hatch and sneak out of the harbor. We should have.

Instead, we spent hours below doing what we do best -- cleaning. We chiseled at the ring around the inside of the toilet bowl, went through two cans of Endust, and magically turned musty odors into pleasant smells.

We were proud of our wizardry. The boat owner was appalled! His interior was **too** clean.

This unhappy event taught us early on that one person's eyesore may be another's delight. If you are a boat owner thinking about having someone maintain your interior, tell them before they start what you are comfortable with. If you are going to be doing the cleaning -- ask. This should apply to the exterior as well. Being up-front at the beginning is better than being in an uncomfortable situation at the end.

Stand By For Efficiency Below
Make a list of supplies you will need for a particular interior. Keep them together in a caddy.

Save steps by cleaning one room at a time.

Take your caddy brimming with cleaning supplies by the handle and go into one room. Clean the entire room. Go to the next room and do the same. Start aft and work your way forward or vice versa.

Cleaning one room at a time is not only efficient, but you will have more energy when you are through to go topside and pick a fight with a sea gull.

Windows/Mirrors

Same as the exterior. Vinegar and fresh water for glass and plastic polish for the plastic ports. Some mirrors are also made of plastic.

Vacuum and lubricate runners if needed. Do not forget about the glass on clocks, barometers, and control panels. Little details make a big difference.

Curtains

Vacuum on a regular basis. Most curtains can be dry cleaned or machine washed under a delicate cycle.

If during a rain storm, water spots beat you to the curtains before you close the windows, here's what you should do: Place a damp rag under the spot and rub area with another damp rag from the other side working from the center of the stain outward.

Upholstery

Vacuum periodically. Take cushions off and vacuum underneath for crumbs and cobwebs. Wipe up spills with detergent and fresh water before they dry.

Carpet

The more a carpet is walked on, the more it should be vacuumed. If not, the dirt and sand will grind into the fibers and wear it down.

Keep some commercial spot remover handy. Most brands work pretty well. Wipe up the little spots before they turn into one gigantic one.

If the carpet is already bad, hire a professional to clean it. If you are the type that likes to go to Von's and rent a carpet cleaning machine, be sure you get all the water up from the carpet. Water attracts dirt like a magnet attracts metal.

Do Yourself a Favor: Scotchgard

If you are tired of seeing little Joey's Coke soak into the furniture and carpet, Scotchgard it. Scotchgard is a fabric protector and the greatest invention next to the boat. It is an interior's guardian angel because it makes little beads out of foreign liquid matter which allows you to wipe it up before it dries into the fabric.

Read the manufacturer's directions and warnings on the back of the can.

The Galley

This is one area where it is better to throw away a mess rather than have to clean it up. Take some aluminum foil and line the shelves in the refrigerator, the bottom of the oven, and the stove top.

Refrigerator: Clean with white vinegar. Doing so will cut grease, kill mildew, and remove odors. There is no need to rinse.

If the refrigerator is not going to be used for a while, turn the unit off and leave the door open for ventilation. Secure the open door so it does not close or cause damage.

Stainless Steel Sinks: These sinks should be kept like the outside of the boat: clean, dry, and waxed.

Rust can usually be found in this area, but it is not the sink's fault. The rust is caused by leaving metal utensils in the sink. To remove rust, use a mild abrasive or a rust remover. Flush with detergent and fresh water.

Counter Tops: Wipe down with detergent and fresh water, then dry. Going over this surface with Endust creates a shiny-clean effect to young and old counter tops alike.

The Head

Clean the head, shower, and basin with liquid Lysol. Waxing the toilet bowl and shower after they

Combat interior mildew by circulating a fan and leaving a light on.

are dry will keep them clean and make maintenance easier. Put a rubber mat in the shower after waxing.

Pour about a cap full of liquid Lysol into the toilet bowl to help combat odors. Spray the entire area with Lysol spray to help prevent mildew.

Vinyl Overheads

Imagine being sentenced to life as a vinyl overhead: You cannot move. From below comes clouds of cigarette smoke, the cooking odors of a bad cook and every once in a while you are hit by a flying champagne cork. You begin to turn yellow because the life as a vinyl overhead is not worth living.

Nothing can keep you from this natural deterioration process, but something can slow it down: a good vinyl cleaner/restorer.

Varnished Trim

Trim that has been finished is virtually maintenance free and should last for years if the wood beneath it does not get wet. Wipe occasionally with Endust or any good furniture polish.

Unfinished Trim

Liquid Gold works great on bare wood. It cleans and oils at the same time. We also found that Liquid Gold hides a lot of flaws in the wood. If you want something that is going to harden, use linseed oil. Do not use dressings meant for exterior use. They contain strong volatiles that will get you if they cannot get fresh air.

Lurking Mildew

Are the eyes of mildew upon you? If they are, it is because there are some damp, dark, musty, places to hide such as drawers and bulkheads.

Eliminate the mildew with X-14 mildew remover. Test an inconspicuous area first. Then get yourself a small fan and a light bulb for the interior. The fan will keep the air circulating, but be sure to secure it so it cannot fall. The light bulb is for dry heat. If your boat is docked, it is a good idea to have the electrical dock

Mates, leave your dirt at the door.

supply checked for leakage by a professional. This will help to eliminate electrolytic corrosion. (For more details, see Chapter 11, A Tip Tip Bottom.)

When the boat is not in use, open compartments and take out any wet articles like life jackets. To keep clothes and linens fresh on the boat, place fabric softener sheets in the drawers and closets.

Odors Down Under

To freshen the air, set a bowl(s) of vinegar out while the boat is taking a break from entertaining. Be sure that the bowls are secure and the vinegar cannot spill from them.

Leave Dirt at the Door

Place a vinyl/rubber backed mat in front of the entrance to the interior with a sign above it that reads: "Wipe 'em off or take 'em off."

Cannot Blame it on the Sun

Protect the interior from the sun's ultra violet rays by installing window covers, or pull the curtains shut when the boat is just sitting.

The little energy spent in protecting your boat's interior will save you from having to replace a teak veneer dash and/or faded carpet which could cost you untold dollars.

11

A TIP TOP BOTTOM

Sher's definition of below the waterline maintenance: *"Helping metal hardware, fiberglass, and wood survive life submerged in a giant battery."*

The two most important reasons to keep the bottom of your boat properly cleaned and thoroughly inspected are safety and performance.

For safety's sake, the middle of the ocean is not the place you want to be when you learn that your boat has a cracked prop. Imagine your wife, or someone dear to you, having to do the last three miles to Catalina dog paddling.

In terms of performance, if there is growth clinging to the hull of your boat, it can cut down your fuel consumption anywhere from five to thirty percent, depending upon the amount of growth.

The bottom line is: Do not let down your bottom, because it is liable to do the same to you out in the midst of nowhere.

A Fish's Eye View

The greatest disadvantage a boat owner has with an underwater service is the inability to check the work.

Wouldn't it be great if we could jump into the bay, turn into fishes just as we hit the water (like Mr. Limpet) and watch our divers do their thing?

Let us pretend, for just a moment, that we can do just that -- be fishes incognito. If the diver in front of

If you are unable to find a fish to spy on your diver, ask your bottom service to provide you with a video inspection of your boat's bottom.

us servicing the sailboat is a true professional, he should be able to pass the checklist below:

[ ] He is equipped with the following supplies: a stainless steel sponge, a scraper with a stiff blade, a piece of thick carpet, a Scotch-Brite pad, a screw driver, and (of course) a source of air supply.

[ ] If he is wearing tanks, he knows to always face the boat so he won't damage the hull with them.

[ ] He uses his wet suit for buoyancy and adjusts his weights so he is pressed up against the hull about forehead level. He doesn't fight to stay down or sink to the bottom.

[ ] The professional always cleans by sight not by touch.

[ ] He cleans by using vertical/horizontal motions as opposed to circular.

[ ] He uses the least abrasive material he can to clean the hull.

[ ] As he cleans the hull, he clears the through hulls, the knot meter, the raw water-intake valve, and the depth sounder of any growth that might be blocking their openings.

[ ] He checks the hull for blisters and the metal hardware for cracks and electrolysis.

[ ] He studies the zinc carefully for corrosion and will replace only if necessary.

[ ] He polishes the prop and shaft with his stainless steel sponge.

[ ] After he is done, he swims the hull again to double check his work.

Unfortunately, our being fish, watching a diver clean the bottom of our boat is all make-believe. But the list is a reality and had better be for all professional divers. (Maybe Mr. Limpet would like a spying job working for the federation of boat owners?)

How Often

In conditions like we have here in Southern California, every seventy-two hours something microscopic drops anchor on the hull of a boat and starts to grow there. In the winter it is less.

With the exception of wood boats, professionals suggest that the bottoms be serviced every month during the summer and every other month during the winter, provided the boats are kept in the water.

Wooden boats should be serviced less because of their softer paint: Every other month during the summer and every three to four months during the winter. It really depends on the area you are in and its growth rate.

"The Dry Diver"

This is a device which allows the boat owner to clean the bottom of his boat without getting wet. The instrument is composed of a series of scrub brushes with foam floats attached to them. The device conforms to the side of the hull and when pushed down into the water, tries to force its way back up causing a scrubbing-like action. It can be found in most marine hardware stores for about $80.00. It is a good idea if you only want half the job done.

When it comes right down to it, it is far better to have a wet professional diver than an amateur dry one. These are my reasons:

1) You stay dry but you cannot see what you are cleaning.
2) The "Dry Diver" does only a marginal job.
3) The "Dry Diver" does not give you a personal inspection of the hull and hardware.
4) The "Dry Diver" does not know how to change a prop.
5) The "Dry Diver" does not know what electrolysis looks like, nor could it tell you if it did.

"Bagging" Your Boat

This is not the system for the boat owner who just wants to get on his boat, start the engine, and get the heck away from reality.

The procedure is such that the boat would actually be sitting in a bag filled with chemicals preventing bottom growth and a quick escape. Every time you wanted to use the boat, you would have to untie the bag, drive the boat out, and tie the bag again. I understand it works well, but is not worth the inconvenience.

There has also been some concern expressed by the Environmental Protection Agency (E.P.A.) that the bags may be polluting the water. Either by the chemicals or by the bag sinking to the bottom of the bay and being left to deteriorate into unhealthy tidbits for marine life. Studies are still being done.

A Layman's Look at Electrolysis

In my attempt to understand a phenomenon such as electrolysis (the corrosion of metals), I had to keep reminding myself that the problem was caused by two totally different sources: one, a giant God given battery which will never die (unless man kills it) and two, a man-made electrical source which will never survive (unless man keeps it alive).

Galvanic Corrosion: This corrosion is caused by the giant God given battery -- the ocean.

When two dissimilar metals are placed into this sea of energy, an electrical current is generated between them and the birth of corrosion is the result.

The weaker of the metals (the *base* metal) will dissolve so that the stronger metal (the *noble*) will survive and do the job it is intended to do.

Electrolytic Corrosion: This corrosion is caused by a man-made electrical current which has gone awry or "stray".

These wandering destructive currents usually emerge from an external source such as the boat's battery or shore power supply with a poorly installed electrical circuit.

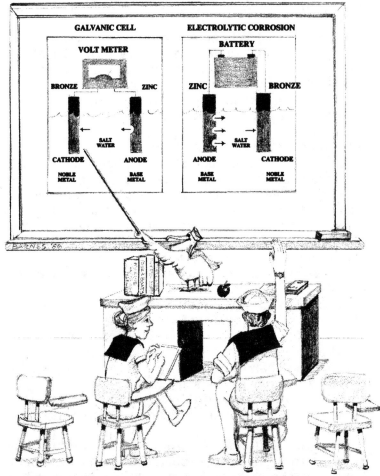

A brief education in electrolysis (the corrosion process of metals) will help to provide longer lives to metal hardware.

Larger powerboats, and any boat which happens to be docked next to them, suffer greatly from this corrosion due to their need to run more electricity than most sailboats.

Electrolytic corrosion is stronger than galvanic corrosion in that it will drive a more noble metal to corrode which normally would not under galvanic conditions.

The most critical point to be made about electrolytic corrosion is that one must be aware that the stray current can either be dribbling, like a stream or gushing, like a waterfall.

The Recipe for Corrosion (Serves Millions)

An Electrolyte (The ocean. It can conduct electricity.)

A Cathode (A noble metal)

An Anode (A base metal)

This recipe works best when the electrolyte is warm and salty, fresh water won't do. Because we are using the ocean as out electrolyte, it moves naturally and produces a great electrical current. Add the cathode and anode, bronze and zinc are favorites, to the electrolyte and bond them together. Corrosion will flow. Variations can be made as to which cathode and anode to use, but it is imperative that the correct ones be chosen. (See Galvantic Survivors and Protectors on page 114.)

This recipe is disliked all over the world.

Cathodic Protection

If we didn't have the anodes to protect the cathodes from corrosion, we would all be like the little Dutch boy with his finger in the side of the dam trying to keep it from bursting.

There are a number of methods used today, but the most popular is the use of a *sacrificial anode*. A sacrificial anode is a base metal purposely connected to a noble metal (or the cathode) to protect it. The sacrificial anode will gradually corrode while protecting the cathode.

Galvantic Survivors and Protectors

High-Chromium Stainless Steel
Nickel-Copper Alloy
Copper-Nickel Alloy
Bronze (popular "noble" metal)
Copper
Brass
Tin
Lead
Lead-Tin Soldier
Low-Chromium Stainless Steel
Cast Iron
Wrought Iron
Mild Steel
Cadium
Aluminum
Zinc (most commonly used "base metal")
Magnesium

This is a list of metals most commonly used in the boat-building industry. They are listed in order of their ability to resist corrosion in saltwater. Starting from the top with the noble metals which survive electrolysis when they are protected by the base metals below. For example, if zinc and bronze are joined together (bonded) then the zinc will corrode to save the bronze.

The most common sacrificial anode used is zinc because it corrodes most rapidly in salt water. This is the way the process works: the sacrificial anode is electrically joined to a noble metal, such as bronze. For example, placing a zinc rudder disc to a bronze rudder. The zinc will corrode while the bronze rudder is protected. When the zinc is consumed it must be replaced.

The life of the zinc depends on the area in which the boat is docked.

Oddly enough, zinc is the least expensive of all the metals but can save you the most money. For instance, a prop can cost hundreds of dollars, whereas, installing zinc to preserve it only costs pennies.

Preventing Electrolytic Corrosion

Preventing this type of corrosion is a matter of good electrical wiring. For your sake, and your neighbors, have a professional technician come out and survey your boat for possible electrical leakage.

They are equipped with a sensitive meter which will tell them immediately if you have an electrical leak. They can also check your shore power supply.

Discouraging Galvanic Corrosion

Because galvantic corrosion is a natural event and not man-made, it will be around for many years. If we want to continue to enjoy boating, we must continue to control this process by:

1) Attempting to make all parts of an item from the same metal.
2) If metals need to be mixed, which is usually the case, make the more important items, like the fastenings, the more noble metals.
3) Electrically insulate the different metals.
4) The "anode" must be thick enough to allow for corrosion.
5) Make yourself aware of any stray currents from your boat and your neighbor's boat.
6) Do not paint the anode. It will not corrode if you do.
7) Do not paint metal hardware. It cannot be inspected properly.

Fresh Water Scum

Fresh water is less conductive than salt water and hence, causes little corrosion if any.

But fresh water can cause hard water build-up if the boat is left in the water for a prolonged period of time or is not hosed off after being taken out of the water.

If compounding does not remove the build-up, try Lime Away or miriatic acid. Test an inconspicuous area first and use plenty of fresh water.

The Boat Owner vs. The Professional Diver

Whether you clean the bottom of the boat yourself or hire a professional, it is best to know what is going on. The bottom of your boat is the last thing to be uneducated about.

If you are looking to hire a diver, here are some guidelines to follow before you trust him with your bottom:

1) How long has he been diving/cleaning?
2) Ask for references and follow through with phone calls to those people.
3) Ask reputable boatyards for advice and assistance. (After all, they see bottoms all the time.)
4) Ask the diver to define electrolysis and its prevention.
5) Ask the diver to explain his cleaning procedure and tools used.

12

DOCK RAT BITS

Sher's definition of dock rat bits: *"Little pieces of advice taken from the mouths of waterfront authorities."*

The following quotes have been graciously given by all different sorts of "dock rats": boat maintenance workers; boat owners; divers; sail cleaners; and boat brokers, to name a few. I found these people scurrying about such harbors as Newport Beach, Long Beach, San Pedro, Friday Harbor and Nanaimo, B.C., Canada.

These words of wisdom were given in an effort that you might learn from their experience instead of, perhaps, learning the hard way which sometimes comes from our own mistakes.

"In today's world of yachts, the appearance of canvas work has become increasingly important. The function of boat covers is many times placed in a secondary role. Proper canvas work where function is not forgotten can save a boat owner untold dollars in maintenance costs and add dramatically to the life of varnish work and other sun sensitive areas of your boat. Cover up! Good canvas work is worth every dollar you pay for it."

– Don Thomas, V.P., General Manager
Blinn & Young, Inc., Newport Beach, CA

"As a boat maintenance worker, the best advice I can give to a boat owner is to wash his boat weekly and rinse it down after each use to remove the salt water. Leaving the salt on the boat will eventually cause cosmetic damage. To make the job easier, use such tools as: a squeegee, a nozzle for the hose, an extension pole with a soft scrub brush, and an absorber (synthetic chamois). Remember that all the products you use on your boat roam throughout the bay and eventually flow into our ocean. Try to use biodegradable products whenever possible so that you don't choke the fish and birds."

– Bonnie Haines
Newport Beach, CA

"It has been my experience that maintenance performed on a regular basis, at least once a week, is cruicial if the yacht owner is to avoid costly service expenses due to the normal wear and tear induced by the elements and normal recreational use."

– Robert Dair
Newport Beach, CA

"Maintenance should be considered an additional monthly expense before the purchase of the boat. It is common that the boat owner realizes the extra expense after the fact and finds that it does not fit into his budget which causes his new investment to depreciate rapidly."

– Shari Woodbridge
Laguna Beach, CA

"If you fish out of your boat, continuously rinse it off while you are at sea with a bucket of water from the ocean, and be sure to hose it down good when you return to your dock. If you don't, it makes for a long, hard cleaning job for you or your cleaning crew."

– Lynn Hunter
Long Beach, CA

"If you are curious about the condition of the bottom of your boat and do not want or need to haul it out, ask your diving service to provide you with a video inspection."

– Jose A. Acevedo
Long Beach, CA

"All thru-hull valves should be exercised periodically to keep them working smoothly. Proper maintenance will prolong battery life. Keep batteries clean and topped up with water and DO NOT overcharge them. A good preventive maintenance program will keep your boat in the shape you want it and in the long run, will cost less than remedial maintenance."

– David Tharp
San Diego, CA

"In regard to the Evinrude 9.9 1975-1976 engines, only use Evinrude oil which helps reduce replacement of coils."

– Richard L. Henderson
Nanaimo, B.C., Canada

"If you are not going to be using your boat but will be leaving it in the water, wrap a garbage bag around the leg of the engine to protect it from growth build-up. Put a reminder of some sort next to the ignition switch so you remember to remove it before turning the engine on."

– Pat Johnstone, Tackle & Marina
Nanaimo, B.C., Canada

"Don't leave fishing bait in a refrigerator that has been turned off. The smell it leaves is horrendous and virtually impossible to get rid of."

– Bonnie Johnstone
Nanaimo, B.C., Canada

"Don't hire cheap unsupervised amateurs to do a professional job. You will only end up paying twice for the same job. Once for the unprofessional and then

again for the professional to come out and fix what the amateur should have done correctly in the first place."
— Southern Cross Yacht Systems
Newport Beach, CA

"If you have varnish on your boat, keep it on a ninety to one hundred day maintenance schedule. If you keep it maintained, it won't go bad. The big expense is fixing the neglected varnish, not maintaining the good stuff."
— Bruce Cunard
Newport Beach, CA

"Boat owners should realize the large investment wrapped up in sails and covers. Having them regularly cleaned should be considered preventive maintenance which will save them from costly unforseen damages."
— Aqua Marina
Newport Beach, CA

"Preventive maintenance is the magic number one, but the bottom line is: have lots of money."
— Chuck Reed
Newport Beach, CA

"Let's stay ahead of the game instead of worrying about it until it breaks."
— KC Underwater Yacht Service
Newport Beach, CA

"A boat is like a wife . . .it seemed like a good idea at the time."
— Brian Eckford
Huntington Beach, CA

"Educate yourself so you can relate to the people working on every aspect of your boat. Understanding what they are talking about eliminates you from being buffaloed by them."
— Odessey Diving
Newport Beach, CA

"Since the early seventies, the use of vinyl decal accent stripes has become the most common means of adding color striping to boats. While this method is not as permanent as colors molded in the gel coat, it does have its advantages should the striping be scratched. Scratching across multiple colors of gel coat is very difficult to repair, requires a professional to do, and generally is hard to match the existing gel as it is probably faded. To repair decal striping, you can do the job yourself and get good results following these steps:

1) Using a sharp razor, remove only a small section around the damaged area cutting on a diagonal line across the tape.
2) Peel damaged tape away. If it does not come off easily, use a heat gun or blow dryer to soften the tape. Do not overheat. If tape leaves a glue residue clean with acetone or lacquer thinner.
3) Apply new tape making sure to cut on the same diagonal lines as the old tape was cut. Overlap the tape lightly over the old to allow for shrinkage.
4) The repair is complete. Remember, up close the repair may be noticeable to you, but from a short distance back, the repair will look considerably better than the old scratched material."

– Eric Rankin
Newport Beach, CA

"I find great pleasure in boarding a clean, beautifully maintained boat and pride in showing her off. The only feeling I get from a neglected boat is embarrassment."

– Smitty
Friday Harbor, WA

	JAN	FEB	MAR	APRIL	M
1 **Windows** Glass, Plexiglas, Eisinglass					
2 **Polish Metal** Stainless Steel, Brass & Bronze					
3 **Cushions**					
4 **Lifelines, Fenders, Shore Power Cords**					
5 **Lube Snaps**					
6 **Give a Darn, Lend an Arm**					
7 **Clean & Oil Teak**					
8 **Varnishing**					
9 **Compounding & Waxing**					
10 **Running & Standing Rigging**					
11 **Sails & Covers**					
12 **Bilge**					
13 **Bottom**					
14 **Interiors**					
15					

TO A BEAUTIFUL BOAT

June	July	August	Sept	Oct	Nov	Dec

Good job mates.

INDEX

A
Acrylic floor polish, 75
Aluminum, oxidized, 32
Anchor cable holes, history of, 11

B
Bilge: history of, 11; cleaning, 96; inspecting, 97;
    running after washdown, 24
Bilge pump, history of, 11
Bleach, against mildew, 22
Blocks, 83
Boat: history of, 12-13
Boat bag, 111
Bosun's chair, 76-78
Bottom cleaning: diver's checklist, 109; how often, 110
Brass, 32
Bronze, 32
Brushes: types of, 17

C
Canvas, importance of, 117
Cathodic protection, 113
Chainplates, 81
Chamois, 17, 24
Compounding, 71-74
Control panels, 20
Corrosion: galvantic, 111; electrolytic, 111-113
Covers washing and water-proofing, 91, 92
Cushions: closed-cell foam, 20; details; vinyl, 20

D
Decals, repair of, 121
Detailing, 28-40
Detergents: biodegradable, 19
Diver: duties, 109
Docklines: cleaning, 23; inspecting, 39
"Dry Diver", The, 110
Drying: tools used for, waterways, 24